SPECIAL OPERATION FORCES BUG-IN SURVIVAL BIBLE

Create a Resilient, Impenetrable Home Defense and Ensure
Your Family's Safety in Any Case of Emergency

NATE COLTON

Disclaimer

This book is intended for informational purposes only. The content within reflects the author's research, personal opinions, and understanding of the topics discussed. It is not a substitute for professional advice. The author and publisher assume no responsibility or liability for any injury, loss, or damage incurred as a consequence, directly or indirectly, from the use or application of any of the contents of this book. The reader is advised to consult appropriate professionals before taking any actions based on the information contained in this book.

All emergency and disaster preparedness strategies presented in this book are subject to interpretation, and real-world outcomes may vary depending on individual circumstances. The author does not guarantee the success or safety of any method discussed. Readers are responsible for their own safety and the safety of others in any crisis or disaster situation.

All efforts have been made to ensure that the information in this book is accurate at the time of publication. However, the author and publisher are not liable for any errors, omissions, or inaccuracies, or for any consequences arising from the use of the information in this book.

TABLE OF CONTENTS

INTRODUCTION

WHY BUGGING IN IS THE ULTIMATE DEFENSE STRATEGY

- -

The Importance of Staying Put in a Crisis

In moments of crisis, our natural instinct may often tell us to flee, to seek refuge elsewhere. However, there are numerous scenarios where leaving your home, your stronghold, could expose you and your family to greater danger. Whether it's a natural disaster, civil unrest, or an unexpected threat, "bugging in" — staying put and fortifying your home — is often the most effective and secure option. In fact, the principles used by Navy SEALs in high-risk situations emphasize preparedness, adaptability, and using one's immediate environment to maximum advantage. In this section, we'll explore why staying home during a crisis can be your safest bet and how it offers unparalleled control and security.

One of the primary reasons for staying in your home during a crisis is the inherent unpredictability of external environments. The world outside, in the midst of chaos, is far more dangerous and unpredictable than the controlled environment within your own walls. Your home is a known space — one that you can prepare, control, and fortify according to your needs. Leaving means relinquishing control, subjecting yourself and your family to dangers that you cannot foresee or manage, such as blocked roads, hostile environments, or the risk of being caught in mass evacuations.

Control Over Your Environment

When you choose to stay put, you immediately gain control over your environment. Everything you need for survival — food, water, medicine, and shelter — is already within your reach. For someone like our buyer persona, Jack, who is highly organized and prepared, staying home offers the ability to implement plans and fortifications he has been building over time. By staying put, you have access to your tools, your fortifications, and your family's preparedness supplies, giving you a substantial advantage over those trying to leave.

Moreover, controlling your environment also means controlling your level of exposure to external threats. In a crisis, crowds can become unpredictable and hostile. In natural disasters, for example, roads become congested, and fuel becomes scarce, leaving you stranded and vulnerable. In civil unrest or widespread panic, being caught in a crowd puts you at the mercy of others' fear and desperation. Staying home eliminates this risk. It provides a space where you can establish clear defensive lines, monitor your perimeter, and maintain your autonomy.

Accessibility to Essential Resources

In a prolonged crisis, the scarcity of resources becomes a primary concern. By staying home, you avoid the risk of running out of food, water, and supplies that can be quickly depleted in evacuation zones. Evacuating typically means leaving behind most of your essential resources and relying on public shelters, which may be ill-equipped to meet everyone's needs. For someone like Jack, who has meticulously planned and stored long-term supplies, staying put ensures that these resources remain available and within reach.

In addition, home-based food and water supplies are often far more reliable than what you could carry with you on the move. If you've stored emergency food that can last for weeks, set up rainwater collection systems, or installed solar panels, staying home allows you to make use of these resources to their fullest extent. On the other hand, the uncertainty of evacuation means you're relying on unpredictable sources for the most basic necessities.

Strategic Home Fortification

One of the most powerful arguments in favor of staying put during a crisis is the ability to fortify your home. Your house becomes your fortress — a safe space that you've already begun to reinforce with security measures, following many of the practical strategies we'll discuss in the coming chapters. Navy SEALs are trained to adapt their immediate surroundings into secure positions, making their environment work to their advantage, and you can do the same.

Whether it's reinforcing your windows and doors, creating safe rooms, or setting up monitoring systems, fortifying your home allows you to take proactive steps to ensure the security of your loved ones. This level of preparation is not possible when you are on the move, with few tools and little protection. A fortified home is a stronghold that keeps you out of harm's way and deters potential intruders or looters. In a crisis, those seeking to take advantage of the chaos will be far more likely to target vulnerable, unfortified homes than those that present clear signs of defense.

Furthermore, staying in a fortified home allows you to manage access. You can control who enters and exits, monitor your surroundings with security cameras or motion detectors, and engage potential threats from a position of strength. This contrasts sharply with being on the road, where you're exposed to unpredictable dangers and where personal security is far harder to maintain.

Familiarity and Psychological Stability

Your home provides more than just physical safety; it also offers psychological comfort in times of crisis. For families like Jack's, who are looking to maintain a sense of normalcy during chaos, staying in a familiar environment can be key to maintaining mental resilience. The Navy SEALs teach the importance of mental fortitude — remaining calm and collected under pressure is half the battle. Staying in a familiar, controlled environment helps reduce stress levels and allows you to think more clearly and make better decisions.

For children, in particular, remaining at home during a crisis can offer the stability they need to stay calm. Uprooting a family during a disaster adds layers of emotional and psychological stress, especially when children are faced with unfamiliar, potentially hostile environments. By staying put, families can focus on working together, using the comfort of home to maintain routines, and minimizing the fear of the unknown. This stability can be crucial in prolonged emergencies, where morale can wane over time.

Avoiding Unnecessary Exposure to Danger

Leaving your home during a crisis can also put you directly in harm's way. From congested roads to exposed shelters, the act of evacuating brings with it a host of dangers that you can avoid by staying put. During natural disasters, roadways often become impassable due to debris or flooding, which could leave you stranded with no access to help. In cases of civil unrest or widespread panic, evacuation zones may become breeding grounds for violence, theft, and unrest.

By choosing to "bug in," you limit your exposure to external dangers. You avoid the unpredictability of other people's actions and the instability of public spaces. Staying home provides you with a known, controlled space that you can defend and maintain, minimizing the potential risks that come with abandoning your stronghold.

How Navy SEALs Tactics Can Be Applied to Home Defense

The Navy SEALs are renowned for their ability to operate in the most extreme environments and under the most dangerous conditions. What makes their tactics so effective is a combination of preparation, adaptability, and the disciplined execution of well-planned strategies. These very tactics can be adapted to home defense, transforming your home into a secure stronghold capable of withstanding a variety of threats — from natural disasters to civil unrest. By adopting these strategies, you can ensure that your home is not just a place of refuge, but a well-fortified fortress that provides real protection for your family.

One of the key reasons Navy SEALs are so successful in their missions is their focus on preparation and planning. Before any operation, SEALs spend significant time gathering intelligence, studying the terrain, and evaluating potential risks. For someone like Jack, the ex-military homeowner described in our buyer persona, this type of preparation comes naturally. However, even without a military background, the principles of detailed planning and situational awareness can be applied effectively to home defense.

Threat Assessment and Situational Awareness

One of the first tactics the Navy SEALs emphasize is threat assessment. Whether preparing for a mission in hostile territory or defending your home from external threats, understanding the environment around you is crucial. In home defense, this means conducting a thorough evaluation of your property and its vulnerabilities. Are there areas that are easily accessible to intruders? Are your windows and doors adequately reinforced? Is the surrounding area prone to natural disasters like flooding or wildfires?

By understanding the specific threats your home might face, you can begin to implement strategies to mitigate these risks. SEALs are trained to constantly assess their environment, staying aware of changes in terrain or potential enemy movements. For you, this could translate to installing security cameras that monitor key entry points, as well as using motion sensors to track movement outside your home. Being aware of your environment means being one step ahead of any potential threat — whether it's a natural disaster or a security breach.

SEALs also use what is called the OODA Loop — a decision-making process that stands for Observe, Orient, Decide, Act. This loop helps them respond quickly and effectively in high-stakes situations. Homeowners can apply the same process to home defense. For example, observing unusual activity outside your home through security systems, orienting yourself by identifying possible dangers, deciding on a course of action (whether to call authorities or fortify certain areas), and then acting swiftly. This cycle is repeated continuously in crisis situations to maintain an edge over any potential threats.

Layered Defense Strategy

Another core principle in Navy SEAL tactics is the concept of layered defense. This tactic involves creating multiple layers of protection to slow down or deter any potential adversary. When it comes to home defense, a layered approach means that no single point of entry is left vulnerable. SEALs use layers to make it difficult for enemies to reach their objective, and you can do the same with your home.

Start with the outermost layer — your property's perimeter. This could involve erecting fences, planting thorny bushes near windows, or setting up motion-activated floodlights that deter anyone from approaching undetected. The next layer involves the house itself: reinforcing doors with deadbolts, securing windows with shatter-resistant glass or security bars, and installing high-quality locks. Finally, the innermost layer is what we call the core defense — this could include creating a safe room or panic room where your family can retreat if the outer defenses are breached. Inside this safe room, you should have emergency supplies, communication devices, and a plan for what to do next.

Incorporating multiple layers of defense doesn't just protect your home physically; it also buys you time. Each layer slows down or stops an intruder, allowing you to assess the situation and take the necessary action — whether that's calling for help or preparing to defend your home.

Fortifying Entry Points

Navy SEALs understand that in any defensive scenario, controlling entry points is critical. In their missions, this often involves securing doors, windows, and other access points that could be exploited by the enemy. Similarly, when defending your home, reinforcing entry points should be a top priority. Doors and windows are the most vulnerable areas of your home, and they need to be fortified to withstand forced entry.

You can apply SEAL tactics by upgrading to steel-reinforced doors, installing heavy-duty deadbolts, and using door barricades that prevent the door from being kicked in. Similarly, windows can be protected with security film that makes them shatter-resistant or by installing security bars that make it impossible for intruders to enter. Just as Navy SEALs ensure that every entry point on their base or compound is secure, your home needs to be fortified in the same way.

For Jack, a buyer persona who is highly invested in DIY solutions, many of these upgrades can be done personally and affordably. Installing reinforced doors and windows is something that can be done over a weekend with the right materials, and the peace of mind that comes with knowing your home is secure is invaluable.

Contingency Plans and Flexibility

One of the hallmarks of Navy SEAL tactics is their ability to adapt to changing situations. In the field, SEALs often have multiple contingency plans in place, allowing them to pivot quickly when unexpected challenges arise. This adaptability is key to surviving in unpredictable environments — and it's equally important for home defense.

When defending your home, it's essential to have backup plans. For example, if your power goes out, do you have alternative sources of energy like generators or solar panels? If intruders disable your primary security system, do you have a secondary system in place, such as battery-operated cameras or a backup power source? Having these contingencies in place ensures that no single point of failure will compromise your home's security.

In addition to contingency plans, SEALs emphasize the importance of training and preparation. They rehearse scenarios repeatedly so that their responses become second nature. For homeowners, this means regularly practicing home defense drills with your family, ensuring that everyone knows how to respond in the event of an emergency. These drills should include plans for evacuation, securing the home, and protecting your loved ones in a safe room.

Psychological Preparation and Resilience

Finally, one of the most important aspects of Navy SEAL tactics is mental resilience. In high-stress situations, staying calm and focused can mean the difference between success and failure. SEALs are trained to manage stress, stay composed, and make rational decisions under pressure. The same mindset applies to home defense. When faced with a crisis — whether it's an attempted break-in or a natural disaster — maintaining a clear head is crucial.

Psychological preparation is often overlooked in home defense, but it's just as important as physical fortifications. Navy SEALs undergo rigorous mental training to ensure they can handle any situation, and as a homeowner, you should adopt the same mindset. Practice mental resilience by preparing yourself for the worst-case scenarios, understanding that your calm and decisive actions will protect your family.

The Benefits of Fortifying Your Home Over Evacuation

In times of crisis, the instinct to leave and find safety elsewhere can be overwhelming. It's natural to want to escape what feels like imminent danger, but evacuation is often fraught with challenges that can place you and your family in more peril than staying put. By fortifying your home, you not only avoid the chaos and uncertainty of the outside world, but you also ensure that you have control over your environment, access to necessary supplies, and a solid defensive strategy. For someone like our buyer persona, Jack, who has the skills and mindset to prepare for the worst, fortifying the home becomes the more logical and secure option over fleeing into uncertainty.

Stability and Control in Uncertain Conditions

One of the greatest advantages of staying in your fortified home is stability. Your home is a controlled environment where you can manage every variable. In a crisis situation, everything outside becomes unpredictable — roads can be blocked, gas stations emptied, emergency services overwhelmed. The logistics of evacuating, especially with family members in tow, can quickly become overwhelming. By contrast, staying in your well-fortified home allows you to maintain control over your surroundings.

When you choose to stay, you are in familiar territory. You know the layout of your home, its strengths and weaknesses, and how to secure it. You've likely invested time and effort in preparing it for emergencies, ensuring that windows, doors, and entry points are fortified. You have supplies, tools, and a plan in place. Evacuating strips away that control, leaving you vulnerable to the unknown. Once you're on the road, you're at the mercy of whatever is happening around you, be it natural disasters, civil unrest, or the desperate actions of others.

Control, especially in high-stress situations, is critical. Navy SEALs know that the key to success in a mission is controlling as many variables as possible. The same logic applies to home fortification. When you stay in your fortified home, you are managing the environment, rather than being subjected to the chaos outside. You dictate the terms of your safety. In contrast, evacuation often places you in unpredictable situations where your safety relies on external factors, many of which you can't influence or prepare for.

Access to Essential Supplies

In any crisis scenario, access to basic supplies like food, water, and medical care is essential. By staying in your home, you have immediate access to the supplies you've stored and prepared. If you've taken the time to stockpile food, ensure access to clean water, and secure medical supplies, your home becomes a self-sufficient stronghold. Leaving those supplies behind to evacuate exposes you to the risk of running out of essentials.

Evacuation, on the other hand, forces you to rely on what you can carry. Even if you prepare a well-thought-out bug-out bag, it will never match the comprehensive storage you have at home. In a crisis, resources outside of your home — from food to fuel to shelter — become scarce quickly. Shelters and evacuation zones can become overcrowded and ill-equipped to handle the needs of everyone arriving, which may put you in direct competition with others for limited resources.

For someone like Jack, who values preparation and has invested time into ensuring his home is stocked with long-term supplies, staying home ensures that his family's needs are met. Fortifying the home provides a layer of security that goes beyond physical defense — it also means continued access to essential supplies that are critical for survival in prolonged crises. The peace of mind that comes from knowing you have what you need cannot be overstated.

Security Against External Threats

Another major benefit of fortifying your home is the security it provides against external threats. In times of civil unrest or mass panic, evacuation routes can become extremely dangerous. Highways can be clogged with vehicles, making movement slow and frustrating, while others may see you as a potential target if they are desperate for supplies or transportation. By staying in your fortified home, you minimize the risk of encountering such dangers.

Your home, if properly fortified, can become a defensive stronghold. With the right preparations — reinforced doors, shatter-proof windows, perimeter defenses, and security systems — you can keep intruders at bay and protect your family from outside threats. Navy SEALs operate with the principle that securing a base of operations is essential. You can apply the same principle to your home. Rather than exposing your family to the dangers of the road or an unfamiliar environment, staying put allows you to implement defensive strategies designed specifically for your home's layout and weaknesses.

Additionally, fortifying your home discourages would-be attackers. A fortified home sends a clear message that you are prepared and capable of defending yourself. Those looking to exploit vulnerable homes during crises will likely pass over a house that is visibly reinforced in favor of easier targets. Intruders tend to look for the path of least resistance, and a well-fortified home, with visible deterrents such as security cameras, motion-activated lights, and reinforced entry points, acts as a psychological barrier to potential threats.

Psychological Benefits of Staying Home

The psychological benefits of staying in a fortified home should not be underestimated. In times of crisis, maintaining a sense of normalcy and stability is crucial for mental well-being, especially for families with children. Uprooting your family and evacuating into the unknown can be extremely stressful, creating anxiety and fear not just in yourself, but in your loved ones. Children, in particular, may find evacuation terrifying, as they are thrust into unfamiliar situations with no clear sense of what's happening or when they will return home.

By staying in your fortified home, you provide your family with a sense of familiarity and security. Even in the face of a disaster, the comfort of home can help mitigate the psychological impact of the crisis. Routine and familiarity play a critical role in keeping morale high, and by remaining in your home, you can establish a sense of order in an otherwise chaotic situation. You can continue to use familiar spaces, maintain routines, and ensure that your family feels safe.

Navy SEALs are trained to maintain mental resilience in high-stress situations, and one of the keys to this is creating a controlled environment. When you stay in your home, you control the space, and with that comes mental clarity and calm. You're not constantly scanning your surroundings for new threats or worrying about where your next meal will come from. You're in an environment that you've prepared and understand, allowing you to focus on making clear, rational decisions.

Avoiding the Chaos of Evacuation Routes

When disaster strikes, evacuation routes often become logistical nightmares. Highways can quickly become gridlocked as thousands of people attempt to leave at once, turning what might normally be a short drive into an hours-long ordeal. In many cases, evacuation orders are issued too late, and people find themselves stuck on the road as the disaster catches up to them. By fortifying your home and choosing to stay, you avoid this chaos entirely.

The unpredictability of evacuation routes can expose you to multiple dangers: fuel shortages, road closures, accidents, or even hostile individuals. The thought of being trapped on a highway in the middle of a crisis with no way to turn back is terrifying, and it's a reality many face during mass evacuations. Staying home eliminates this risk, allowing you to focus your energy on defense and self-sufficiency rather than battling the logistical challenges of evacuation.

What This Book Will Teach You: From Mental Resilience to DIY Fortification

The unpredictable nature of crises demands more than just physical preparedness. To truly protect your home and your loved ones, you need a well-rounded strategy that covers both mental resilience and DIY fortification. This book aims to provide you with a comprehensive toolkit that addresses the psychological and physical aspects of preparedness, ensuring that you and your family are ready to face any challenge that comes your way. By learning to think like a Navy SEAL, you'll develop the mental toughness necessary to stay calm under pressure while also building practical, cost-effective defenses for your home.

This isn't just a guide to putting up barriers or storing supplies — it's about creating a holistic, adaptable mindset that allows you to make quick, effective decisions in times of crisis. Whether you're securing your home against intruders or maintaining morale during a prolonged power outage, the skills taught in this book will help you stay in control, no matter what.

Developing Mental Resilience

Navy SEALs are often regarded as some of the most mentally tough individuals in the world. They are trained to operate in high-stress, life-or-death situations, keeping a level head while chaos erupts around them. This book will teach you how to develop a similar type of mental resilience, crucial for staying calm, focused, and decisive during a crisis. When disaster strikes, panic is your greatest enemy. It clouds judgment, causes irrational decisions, and can jeopardize your safety.

Mental resilience isn't just about staying calm; it's about cultivating an unshakable mindset that allows you to move forward with clarity and purpose. This book will guide you through practical exercises to strengthen your mind, from breathing techniques that help manage stress to visualization strategies that allow you to mentally rehearse different scenarios. Navy SEALs are known to mentally walk through missions before they happen, preparing for every potential outcome. By learning to apply this technique to your own preparedness strategy, you'll be able to anticipate challenges and think two steps ahead, even in the most stressful situations.

You will also learn how to build resilience not just for yourself, but for your entire family. Mental strength isn't something that comes naturally to everyone, and in a crisis, the emotional stability of your family members is just as important as your own. This book will show you how to teach resilience-building exercises to your spouse and children, helping them stay calm under pressure and become active participants in your preparedness plan. This isn't just about surviving — it's about thriving, no matter the adversity you face.

DIY Fortification: Protecting Your Home Without Breaking the Bank

While mental resilience forms the psychological backbone of your preparedness, DIY fortification is what makes your home a physical bastion of safety. Unlike expensive professional solutions, the DIY projects outlined in this book are affordable, practical, and effective. These are not overcomplicated, technical projects — they are designed to be achievable with basic tools and materials, so anyone, regardless of their experience level, can implement them.

Fortifying your home starts with understanding its vulnerabilities. This book will teach you how to conduct a thorough home security assessment, identifying weak points that need attention. From flimsy doorframes to unsecured windows, you'll learn how to transform potential entry points into impenetrable barriers. Navy SEALs are trained to see the potential weaknesses in any environment, and this same skill can be applied to your home, ensuring that every door, window, and perimeter is fortified.

You'll learn how to strengthen doors with DIY door reinforcements, using simple materials like steel plates and high-quality deadbolts. Windows, often the weakest point in any home, can be secured with shatter-resistant films and bars that can be installed with minimal cost and effort. For the perimeter of your property, the book provides step-by-step instructions on how to build fences, barriers, and natural defenses that deter intruders without turning your home into a fortress that feels closed off from the world.

Long-Term Sustainability and Resource Management

Beyond the physical aspects of fortification, this book also delves into the long-term sustainability of your home. Protecting your family during a crisis is about more than just locking the doors — you need to ensure that your home can function independently from external resources like power grids and water supplies. This book will guide you through DIY projects that help you achieve energy independence, from installing solar panels to setting up rainwater collection systems.

You'll learn how to create a stockpile of essential supplies that can sustain your family for weeks or even months. From food storage solutions to water purification techniques, this book offers practical advice on how to build and maintain a self-sufficient home. Each project is designed to be affordable, so you don't have to invest a fortune to keep your family safe and secure. These DIY solutions aren't just temporary fixes — they are long-term investments in your family's well-being.

Practical Defense Strategies for Real Threats

In addition to fortifying your home and building a stockpile of supplies, you will also learn defense strategies to protect against real-world threats. Whether you're preparing for a natural disaster, civil unrest, or a home invasion, this book teaches you practical tactics that can be deployed in various scenarios. Navy SEALs operate under the principle that the best defense is a well-planned offense, and the same logic can be applied to home defense.

You'll learn how to set up early warning systems around your property, using affordable technology like motion sensors, cameras, and alarms to detect threats before they reach your doorstep. By establishing clear defensive perimeters, you can monitor the situation from a position of strength, responding quickly and decisively. The book also covers self-defense techniques that you can use to protect your family if an intruder breaches your home. These are not complex martial arts moves but simple, effective tactics that anyone can learn and apply in a moment of crisis.

Building a Preparedness Plan That Works for Your Family

Finally, this book will teach you how to personalize your preparedness plan to fit the unique needs of your family. Every household is different, and what works for one may not work for another. Navy SEALs are experts at creating flexible, adaptable plans that take into account the unpredictability of real-world scenarios. You'll learn how to apply this same mindset to your home defense strategy, creating a plan that is both comprehensive and adaptable.

You'll be guided through the process of creating monthly preparedness checklists that keep your plan up to date. From rotating supplies to testing your security systems, these checklists ensure that nothing is overlooked. Additionally, the book will show you how to run family drills that prepare everyone for a variety of scenarios, from natural disasters to home invasions. By practicing these drills, you ensure that your family knows exactly what to do in a crisis, reducing panic and confusion.

Preparing Your Family for the Unexpected: A Holistic Approach

Preparing for the unexpected is not just about building walls, securing supplies, or setting up surveillance systems — it's about creating a holistic approach that involves the entire family. In any crisis, each member of the household must understand their role and feel confident in their ability to act quickly, calmly, and effectively. A truly effective preparedness plan focuses not only on physical safety but also on mental and emotional resilience, communication, and teamwork. This chapter will guide you through creating a comprehensive plan that prepares your family to face any situation — together.

To create a fortified household ready for any emergency, we must go beyond the practical aspects of home security and incorporate mental, emotional, and strategic preparedness. This means ensuring that every family member, from the youngest to the oldest, knows exactly what to do and feels empowered to contribute. A Navy SEAL approach to crisis management is not just about individual strength but about the power of the team. In this case, your family is the team, and together, you are stronger and more capable of facing the unexpected.

Building Confidence Through Knowledge and Training

One of the key elements in preparing your family for the unexpected is education. Knowledge is power, and in a crisis, being informed about what to do can make all the difference. For adults like Jack, who may already have a strong sense of self-reliance, it's critical to pass on this knowledge to the rest of the family. Children, especially, may feel fear or anxiety in the face of a disaster, but this can be mitigated by teaching them exactly what to expect and how to act.

This book will guide you through how to hold family meetings where you discuss potential threats, evacuation routes, and safety protocols. These meetings should not be seen as panic-inducing but as opportunities to empower your family. Use these moments to educate everyone on how to use emergency equipment, how to contact one another if separated, and how to handle different scenarios, from fires to home invasions to natural disasters.

Practicing Preparedness Together

Having a plan is one thing, but executing that plan under pressure requires practice. It's not enough for each family member to know their role on paper — they need to be able to put it into action confidently. Practicing drills for various emergencies helps solidify the knowledge they've gained and allows them to respond quickly when time is of the essence. Think of it as training for a mission, much like Navy SEALs do.

Start by running family drills for specific scenarios. For example, if there's a fire, everyone should know the fastest way to get out of the house, where to meet, and how to communicate if someone is missing. Similarly, if an intruder tries to break in, each family member should have a role in the household's defense or evacuation, depending on the situation. Drills should be conducted regularly, not just as one-time events, and should be adjusted as children grow older or as household dynamics change.

These exercises will reduce panic in the real event of an emergency. Confidence comes from preparation, and preparation comes from practice. The more familiar each family member is with their role, the less likely they are to feel overwhelmed by fear when a crisis arises.

Creating Mental and Emotional Resilience

In addition to physical preparedness, mental and emotional resilience plays a critical role in how well your family can handle a crisis. Navy SEALs are trained to stay calm under pressure, and a big part of that is their mental preparation. While you may not be training for combat, the principle remains the same: if you can keep your mind clear and your emotions steady, you are far more capable of making smart, quick decisions.

This book will show you how to incorporate stress-management techniques into your family's preparedness routine. Breathing exercises, mindfulness, and even visualization can help everyone in your household manage anxiety during a crisis. Teaching these techniques to your family, especially children, can make them feel more in control of their emotions when things feel out of control around them.

It's also important to ensure that your family has ways to stay emotionally connected during times of crisis. Stress can fracture relationships, but it can also strengthen them if managed correctly. Include emotional check-ins as part of your preparedness drills. This could mean sitting down with your family after a drill or after discussing a new potential threat to make sure everyone is feeling calm and supported. Encouraging open communication helps reduce stress and builds a sense of unity.

Establishing Clear Communication

In any emergency, communication is key. Your family needs to know how to stay in touch if separated and how to get help when needed. This is where a clear, reliable communication plan becomes essential. As part of your holistic preparedness strategy, this book will guide you through creating a family communication plan that includes multiple forms of contact. Relying solely on mobile phones during a crisis can be risky, as networks can become overloaded or go down entirely.

Teach your family how to use radios, walkie-talkies, or other alternative communication devices. Set up clear rendezvous points where family members can meet if they are separated during an emergency. For example, if a natural disaster makes it impossible to stay in your home, you should all have a pre-arranged meeting point where you can regroup safely.

In your home, ensure that each family member has access to emergency contact lists with phone numbers for local authorities, neighbors, and extended family members who may be able to help. Make sure these contact lists are kept in easily accessible locations, like on the refrigerator or next to the landline phone if you have one.

Involving the Whole Family in Preparedness

A truly holistic approach to preparedness means that everyone has a role to play. This is not about one person shouldering the entire burden of responsibility, but about working together as a team. Just as Navy SEALs function as a unit, each family member must understand that they have a role in ensuring the household's safety. Even young children can be taught simple tasks, like how to find the nearest adult or how to use a whistle to signal for help.

Delegating responsibilities ensures that everyone feels invested in the preparedness plan. For instance, older children can be responsible for packing emergency kits, while younger ones can focus on memorizing the family's meeting points. Adults, meanwhile, can ensure that security systems are functioning and that supplies are regularly checked and restocked.

You can also involve your family in DIY fortification projects, making preparedness a hands-on, collective effort. Whether it's reinforcing windows or setting up a rainwater collection system, getting everyone involved not only spreads the workload but also instills a sense of ownership and responsibility in each family member.

CHAPTER 1
HOME SECURITY AND FORTIFICATION

Assessing the Current Security of Your Home

Before you begin fortifying your home, it's essential to understand exactly where you stand in terms of security. Assessing the current security of your home involves looking at your property with a critical eye, identifying vulnerabilities, and recognizing the strengths you can build upon. This initial assessment is the foundation of any effective fortification strategy, and without it, you risk investing time and effort in the wrong areas. Much like a Navy SEAL would survey the terrain before any mission, your first task is to get a clear, unbiased view of your home's defenses.

While you might feel your home is secure because you lock the doors at night and have a basic alarm system, the truth is that most homes have hidden weaknesses that only become apparent under scrutiny. From poorly reinforced doors to outdated windows, many houses are designed for convenience and aesthetics, not for defense. For someone like Jack, our buyer persona who's skilled in DIY and home construction, this process is an opportunity to apply his practical skills. However, even without technical expertise, anyone can conduct a thorough assessment with the right guidance, ensuring their home can withstand whatever threats arise.

Understanding Key Vulnerabilities

To properly assess your home's security, you first need to understand what makes a home vulnerable. The reality is, no matter how safe your neighborhood may feel, your home is likely to have entry points that can be exploited by intruders. The most common vulnerabilities are doors, windows, and the perimeter, but even seemingly insignificant details like landscaping and lighting play a role in home security.

Doors are the primary entry point for most homes, and they are often the weakest link. If your front door isn't reinforced or is made from hollow-core wood, it can be kicked in with minimal effort. Many homeowners don't realize that a standard doorframe offers very little resistance to force, and the locks themselves are often only as strong as the frame holding them. When assessing your home, ask yourself: Can this door withstand a determined attempt to break through it? If the answer is no, that's an immediate area to focus on.

Windows are another critical vulnerability, especially on the ground floor. They may be easier to break than doors, and once shattered, offer a quick and silent entry for intruders. Older homes with single-pane windows or outdated locks are especially susceptible. During your assessment, take a close look at your windows: How easily could someone gain access through them? Are there areas where windows are hidden from view, making it easier for intruders to break in without being noticed?

The perimeter of your home, including your yard, fences, and gates, also plays a crucial role in your overall security. A weak perimeter allows potential intruders to get close to your house without being detected, giving them the time they need to find a vulnerability and exploit it. When assessing the perimeter, look at things like fence height, visibility from the street, and whether there are any blind spots where someone could approach without being seen.

These are the most obvious vulnerabilities, but a comprehensive assessment will also include elements you might not initially consider — like garage doors, which are often overlooked but can be a significant entry point, or crawl spaces that could allow access to the home from beneath. Every part of your home that leads to the outside world needs to be examined through the lens of security.

Assessing Threats Based on Location

While the physical weaknesses of your home are important, you must also consider the location-specific threats that might impact your security. A home in a suburban area like Jack's, for example, faces different risks than a house in a rural or urban setting. In suburbs, there's a higher likelihood of home break-ins due to the proximity of homes to one another, while rural homes might be more vulnerable to intruders because of the isolation and delayed response times from law enforcement.

Start by analyzing your neighborhood's general crime rates. This information is usually available through local police departments or online resources. If there has been an increase in burglaries or break-ins, that's a clear sign you need to heighten your security measures. Even if your area is considered relatively safe, it's crucial to prepare for unpredictable events such as natural disasters, civil unrest, or economic downturns, all of which can increase the risk of crime.

Next, think about the specific geographic risks that come with where you live. Are you in an area prone to flooding, wildfires, or earthquakes? These environmental factors will influence not just how you fortify your home, but how you protect it during these events. For instance, homes in flood-prone areas need more than just physical fortification — they require waterproofing, drainage solutions, and higher ground-level defenses.

Mapping Your Home's Weak Points

Once you've identified general vulnerabilities and considered location-specific threats, it's time to get granular. Create a detailed map of your home that highlights every entry point, including doors, windows, the garage, and any other access points. Take note of which areas seem most exposed or vulnerable, as well as those that are naturally more secure (such as upper-level windows).

Look beyond just the physical structure — map out the sightlines around your property. Where can an intruder approach undetected? Are there bushes, trees, or other landscape features that provide cover? Are there dark areas at night that are not illuminated by streetlights or motion-activated lighting?

This process might take time, but it's an essential step. Once you've mapped out your home's weak points, you'll have a visual representation of your current security standing. This allows you to prioritize where fortifications are most needed and helps ensure no area is left unprotected.

Identifying Immediate Fixes vs. Long-Term Projects

Not every vulnerability you discover during your home assessment will require immediate action. Some areas, such as adding reinforced locks or securing windows with shatter-resistant film, can be handled relatively quickly and affordably. These are what we'll call immediate fixes — high-impact, low-cost improvements that significantly enhance your home's security in a short amount of time.

On the other hand, there will likely be some larger, more complex projects that require careful planning and investment, such as building a perimeter fence or upgrading to hurricane-resistant windows. These are your long-term projects, which will provide greater security over time but may require saving up or gradually working toward completion.

By dividing your home's vulnerabilities into immediate fixes and long-term projects, you can create a phased security plan that prioritizes the most critical issues while still working toward a more comprehensive solution. This approach ensures that your home becomes progressively safer without overwhelming you with all the changes at once.

DIY Fortification Projects on a Budget

Fortifying your home doesn't have to drain your bank account. In fact, with the right approach and a bit of ingenuity, you can transform your home into a secure, impenetrable refuge without breaking the bank. The key is to focus on DIY fortification projects that are both cost-effective and practical. These solutions, designed to enhance your home's security, require minimal investment but yield significant protection. Whether you're protecting against potential intruders or preparing for natural disasters, these projects are perfect for homeowners like Jack, who values self-sufficiency and enjoys hands-on work.

DIY fortifications aren't just about saving money; they are about taking control of your home's security in a personal and empowering way. Instead of relying on expensive contractors or high-tech solutions, you'll be implementing measures that are within your reach and tailored to your specific needs. This chapter will guide you through a series of practical, affordable projects that anyone can implement with basic tools and materials. These projects offer a layer of protection and peace of mind, ensuring your home is ready to withstand any crisis.

Reinforcing Doors: Your First Line of Defense

The front door is often the first point of entry for intruders, which makes reinforcing it a top priority. Many homes, especially older ones, have doors that are easily compromised — either because they are made of hollow-core wood or because their locks are too weak. The good news is that reinforcing your doors can be done at a fraction of the cost of replacing them entirely, and with a little time and effort, you can make this key entry point virtually impenetrable.

Start by installing heavy-duty deadbolts. The standard locks found in most homes are often inadequate when it comes to resisting forced entry. A quality deadbolt, especially one that extends at least an inch into the doorframe, can significantly increase security. For additional reinforcement, consider adding door reinforcement plates, which are metal plates installed around the lock and strike areas of the door. These plates are inexpensive and provide extra resistance against kicking or prying.

Another simple yet highly effective project is installing a door jamb reinforcement kit. These kits strengthen the doorframe, which is often the weakest point of any door, by adding metal plates along the length of the door jamb. A standard wooden doorframe can splinter under pressure, but with this added support, it becomes far more resistant to break-ins.

Finally, consider reinforcing hinges and using longer screws. Swapping out the short screws that come with most hinges for longer, sturdier screws can prevent the door from being easily knocked off its hinges. It's a small and inexpensive change but one that can make a big difference in your home's security.

Securing Windows: Affordable Solutions for Vulnerable Entry Points

Windows are another weak point in many homes, offering easy access for intruders if they are left unsecured. Fortunately, there are several budget-friendly ways to fortify your windows without replacing them entirely. One of the most effective and affordable options is installing security film. This clear adhesive film is applied to the inside of your windows, making the glass much harder to shatter. Even if the window is broken, the film holds the glass together, making it difficult for intruders to gain access.

For windows that are particularly vulnerable, such as those on the ground floor or in secluded areas, consider installing security bars. These bars are often perceived as expensive or unattractive, but many modern designs are affordable, adjustable, and less intrusive. Look for removable or hinged bars that can be easily opened from the inside in case of fire, while still providing a solid barrier against outside threats.

You can also improve the security of your windows by upgrading window locks. Many older homes still have outdated latches that offer little resistance to forced entry. Window pin locks, which are easy to install and inexpensive, allow you to secure your windows in a slightly open position for ventilation without compromising security.

Building Low-Cost Perimeter Defenses

Your home's perimeter is your first line of defense against intruders, and there are several low-cost ways to strengthen it. One of the simplest and most effective strategies is to use landscaping as a deterrent. While a well-kept yard might seem like a purely aesthetic choice, it can also serve a practical purpose in home defense. Thorny bushes or dense shrubs planted near windows create a natural barrier that makes it harder for intruders to approach unnoticed. These plants are affordable, easy to maintain, and add an extra layer of security without any technological investment.

Another budget-friendly project is installing motion-activated lights around your home's exterior. Intruders prefer to operate under cover of darkness, and motion-activated lights can stop them in their tracks. These lights are inexpensive and easy to install, requiring no more than basic tools and minimal time. Place them near entry points, along the perimeter, and in dark corners where intruders might try to hide.

For even more perimeter protection, you can build a DIY fence or reinforce an existing one. While a full-scale fence installation can be costly, using affordable materials like wooden slats or chain-link fencing can provide a significant deterrent without breaking your budget. Add a gravel pathway along the inside of your fence; the noise generated by walking on gravel can serve as an early warning system, alerting you to anyone attempting to breach the perimeter.

Installing Inexpensive Surveillance Systems

In the modern age of home security, surveillance systems don't have to cost a fortune. There are now numerous budget-friendly cameras and monitoring devices that you can install yourself to keep an eye on your property. Wireless, battery-operated cameras with motion detection and night vision capabilities are widely available and can be set up in just a few hours. These cameras can send real-time alerts to your phone, allowing you to monitor your home even when you're away.

Many DIY surveillance systems are modular, so you can start with just one or two cameras and add more over time as your budget allows. Some systems even offer solar-powered options, making them both cost-effective and energy-efficient. Whether you're monitoring the front door, backyard, or side entrances, these cameras offer an extra layer of security without the high costs associated with professional installation.

Maximizing Impact with Minimal Resources

Ultimately, the goal of these DIY fortification projects is to get the most security possible out of minimal resources. By focusing on reinforcing critical entry points, securing vulnerable windows, building affordable perimeter defenses, and installing low-cost surveillance systems, you'll be well on your way to creating a secure, fortified home. The key is to prioritize the most vulnerable areas and tackle these projects one step at a time.

With each improvement, you're not only making your home safer but also gaining the confidence that comes from knowing you've taken control of your security.

Surveillance and Monitoring Systems

When it comes to protecting your home, surveillance and monitoring systems act as your eyes and ears, providing real-time information and peace of mind. In a world where threats can come from both outside and inside your property, setting up a reliable surveillance system is one of the most effective ways to stay one step ahead of any potential intruders. Surveillance isn't just about watching for burglars — it's about creating a comprehensive system that helps you monitor, detect, and respond to any kind of threat, whether it's a break-in, a natural disaster, or even monitoring family safety.

For someone like Jack, who values both practicality and efficiency, a well-designed surveillance system is key. It's not enough to lock the doors and hope for the best; you need the ability to see what's happening outside, identify risks, and take action before the situation escalates. Fortunately, modern technology has made it easier and more affordable than ever to implement a robust surveillance system that doesn't require a professional installation. This chapter will guide you through the basics of setting up DIY surveillance and monitoring systems, from selecting the right equipment to ensuring full coverage of your property.

The Importance of Layered Surveillance

Just like the principle of layered defense that applies to fortifying the physical structure of your home, layered surveillance involves creating multiple levels of monitoring that overlap and support one another. Think of it as creating a security net where no area is left unmonitored. While a single camera might cover your front door, it doesn't provide information about the side yard or back entrances. Relying on only one source of visual information leaves blind spots, and intruders know how to exploit them.

The first step is deciding where to position your cameras for optimal coverage. Start by identifying the high-risk areas of your property — these are usually doors, windows, and any other entry points. You'll want cameras that provide a clear, wide-angle view of these spots, giving you full visibility in the event of a potential breach. Ground-floor windows, garage doors, and side entrances are all critical zones that need monitoring.

Additionally, make sure you have cameras with night vision capabilities, as many break-ins occur under the cover of darkness. Motion-detection cameras are also a smart investment, as they conserve power by only recording when movement is detected, ensuring you capture key moments without wasting storage space.

Next, think about creating a perimeter of monitoring. This means placing cameras along your fence line, driveway, or other outer areas of your property to detect suspicious activity before it even reaches your home. By placing cameras at multiple points, you'll create a security bubble that extends well beyond your front door, giving you the advantage of early detection.

Choosing the Right Equipment

The sheer number of surveillance cameras and monitoring systems available on the market can be overwhelming, but with a little research, you can choose equipment that fits both your budget and your security needs. For homeowners like Jack, who prefer DIY solutions, wireless cameras are often the best option. They're easy to install, don't require professional wiring, and can be controlled remotely via apps or smart home systems.

Look for wireless cameras with the following features:

- High-definition video quality (at least 1080p) to ensure clear images.
- Night vision to capture movement even in low-light environments.
- Wide-angle lenses for maximum coverage of each area.
- Two-way audio so you can communicate with someone at your front door even if you're not home.
- Mobile app integration, allowing you to monitor your home from anywhere.
- Cloud storage or a built-in hard drive to save footage in case you need to review it later.

Many modern surveillance systems also integrate with smart home hubs, allowing you to link cameras, motion detectors, doorbells, and even lights into one cohesive system that you can control from your smartphone or tablet. This level of integration is particularly useful for someone like Jack, who values efficiency and wants to ensure his home is as secure as possible while minimizing the number of devices he has to manage.

For those on a tighter budget, start by installing just a few key cameras at the most vulnerable entry points — like the front and back doors — and add more over time as your budget allows. You can also look for cameras that include solar charging options, reducing long-term costs and ensuring your system stays functional even during power outages.

Adding Motion Detectors and Sensors

While cameras provide invaluable visual information, motion detectors and sensors add another layer of protection by alerting you to movement in real-time. These sensors can be installed at doorways, windows, or any area that's prone to intrusion. When motion is detected, an alert is sent to your phone or security system, allowing you to respond immediately.

A common mistake in home security is relying solely on cameras. While they capture valuable footage, cameras can't always alert you instantly. This is where motion detectors come in. These sensors create a barrier around your home, and as soon as someone crosses it, you'll know. This kind of immediate feedback is critical in crisis situations, where every second counts.

Securing Your Monitoring System

One of the challenges in setting up surveillance and monitoring systems is ensuring that they are tamper-proof. Intruders will often attempt to disable cameras or systems before making their move, which is why it's crucial to secure both the physical equipment and the data it captures. For physical protection, make sure your cameras are placed out of reach, or inside protective housings that shield them from tampering or weather damage.

For digital security, ensure that your cameras are connected to a secure network. Many modern surveillance systems operate through Wi-Fi, which means they are vulnerable to hacking if not properly secured. Change default passwords on all devices, use encryption protocols for your network, and consider setting up a separate Wi-Fi network exclusively for your surveillance system to minimize the risk of unauthorized access.

If your system uses cloud storage, make sure you are aware of how that data is protected and who has access to it. Always opt for two-factor authentication when possible, ensuring that even if your login information is compromised, it's much harder for someone to gain access to your footage.

Integrating Audio and Visual Alerts

Another way to strengthen your surveillance system is by adding audio and visual alerts that actively deter intruders. Many camera systems now offer built-in alarms or audio warnings that can be triggered when motion is detected. This serves two purposes: first, it alerts you immediately to potential threats, and second, it deters would-be intruders who know they've been spotted.

Pairing your cameras with bright, motion-activated lights can further boost the effectiveness of your surveillance system. When an intruder enters the detection zone, the lights flood the area, drawing attention and making it far less likely that they'll continue their attempt.

For Jack and others who want a cost-effective way to deter intruders, these simple additions can make a significant impact. Not only do they provide an immediate response mechanism, but they also help create a sense of constant vigilance — making your home a much less appealing target.

Creating Safe Rooms and Panic Rooms

In times of crisis, having a secure, fortified space within your home can mean the difference between life and death. Safe rooms and panic rooms are designed to protect you and your family from a range of threats, from intruders to natural disasters. Unlike the rest of your home, these rooms are meant to be impenetrable, giving you the peace of mind that no matter what happens outside, you have a haven of safety inside. For someone like Jack, who values being prepared for any eventuality, creating a safe room is a crucial step in fortifying his home.

A safe room or panic room isn't just about having four walls and a door that locks. It's about building a space that can withstand physical attacks, provide essential supplies, and keep you connected to the outside world until help arrives or the threat has passed. This chapter will guide you through the process of creating a safe room that is both practical and cost-effective, without the need for expensive contractors or high-end materials. By focusing on DIY methods and smart choices, you can ensure that your family has a reliable, fortified space to retreat to in the event of an emergency.

Choosing the Right Location for Your Safe Room

The first step in creating a safe room is choosing the right location within your home. Ideally, your safe room should be easily accessible from the main living areas but also hidden enough to avoid detection by potential intruders. Basements and interior closets are popular choices because they offer natural protection from the elements and are often less visible to intruders. However, you'll want to select a space that has strong structural integrity, particularly if your home is in an area prone to natural disasters like tornadoes or earthquakes.

One of the most important factors to consider when choosing the location of your safe room is proximity to sleeping areas. In the event of a nighttime intrusion or sudden disaster, you want to ensure that your family can quickly and easily reach the safe room without having to navigate through dangerous areas of the house. Ideally, the safe room should be close enough to bedrooms so that your family can access it within seconds.

For homes without basements, a reinforced closet or interior room on the ground floor can serve as a safe room. These rooms are not only practical but can be fortified more easily than rooms with multiple windows or exterior walls. The key is to focus on areas of the home that are easy to reach but difficult for an intruder to locate or penetrate.

Fortifying the Structure

Once you've selected the location, the next step is to fortify the structure. The primary goal of a safe room is to create a space that is as impenetrable as possible. This means reinforcing the walls, doors, and any other potential points of entry to ensure that they can withstand both forced entry and external damage.

Start with the door, as this is the most vulnerable entry point. A standard interior door will not offer sufficient protection in the event of a home invasion or disaster. Replace the door with a solid-core door made of heavy materials like steel or reinforced wood. You can also install a steel door frame for added strength, as most doors fail at the frame rather than the lock. For extra security, consider adding multiple locks, including a deadbolt, and reinforcing the hinges with long screws.

The walls of your safe room should also be reinforced. While this can be done by adding layers of drywall or plywood, the most effective DIY solution is to install plywood sheathing or steel plates inside the walls. These materials are affordable and provide a significant barrier against intruders trying to break through. If budget allows, adding ballistic-rated materials or Kevlar panels is another option for those who want the highest level of protection. Keep in mind, however, that even basic reinforcement will significantly improve the room's defenses.

Another aspect of fortification involves ensuring that windows, if present, are properly secured. Ideally, a safe room should have no windows, as they create weak points in the room's defenses. If you must include a room with windows, cover them with security film to make them shatter-resistant or install security bars that prevent entry. These additions may not be impenetrable, but they will buy you valuable time in a crisis.

Stocking the Safe Room with Essential Supplies

A well-fortified safe room is only useful if it has the supplies you need to survive for an extended period. In the event of a long-term crisis or if emergency services are delayed, you want to ensure that you and your family have enough provisions to remain safe and comfortable for several hours or even days.

The basics include water, non-perishable food, and first aid supplies. Store enough water for each family member to last at least 24 hours — ideally, 72 hours if space allows. Water can be kept in large jugs or smaller, individual bottles for ease of use. Non-perishable food items, such as energy bars, canned goods, and dried snacks, should also be stored. Opt for lightweight, high-calorie foods that don't require cooking or refrigeration.

In addition to food and water, your safe room should be equipped with a first aid kit that includes basic medical supplies like bandages, antiseptics, and over-the-counter medications. Depending on the specific threats you're preparing for, you may also want to include prescription medications, extra eyeglasses, or other personal necessities.

Don't forget to include communication devices in your safe room. A fully charged cell phone, portable battery charger, or even a two-way radio can help you stay connected to emergency services or family members outside the home. Many homeowners also opt for emergency radios that receive weather and emergency broadcasts, giving you real-time updates on the situation.

Creating a Plan for Safe Room Use

Creating a safe room is only part of the equation — the other part is ensuring that your family knows exactly how to use it in an emergency. Much like the drills conducted by Navy SEALs to prepare for missions, your family should practice how to access and secure the safe room in a variety of scenarios. Knowing when to retreat to the safe room is just as important as having the room itself.

Set up clear guidelines for when the safe room should be used, whether it's during a home invasion, a severe weather event, or even a chemical hazard. Make sure each family member knows their role — who is responsible for locking the door, who will monitor communication devices, and who will take charge of younger family members or pets.

Practice drills with your family regularly to ensure everyone knows the fastest route to the safe room and can secure the room quickly. These drills should be as realistic as possible, mimicking the conditions of different types of emergencies, such as late-night intrusions or sudden weather events.

Building Perimeter Defenses

Your home's perimeter defense is the first line of security, setting the boundary that separates you from potential threats. By establishing a solid and well-thought-out defense around the outer edges of your property, you create a buffer zone that deters intruders and buys you valuable time in case of an emergency. Navy SEALs often operate with the principle that controlling the perimeter is key to securing a location, and the same logic applies to your home defense strategy. Building a strong perimeter doesn't just enhance security — it sends a clear message to would-be intruders that your home is not an easy target.

For Jack, the buyer persona who is determined to keep his family safe, building a perimeter defense is an essential step in fortifying his home. It's not just about erecting barriers but about creating a multi-layered approach that combines physical obstacles, visual deterrents, and strategic monitoring. By thinking ahead and implementing practical, cost-effective solutions, you can build a comprehensive perimeter defense that significantly boosts your home's security without needing a massive budget.

Understanding the Role of Perimeter Defenses

Before diving into the specifics of building your perimeter defenses, it's important to understand the role these defenses play in your overall security plan. A strong perimeter acts as an early warning system, preventing intruders from easily reaching your home and giving you more time to react. It also serves as a deterrent — most criminals look for easy, vulnerable targets, and a well-defended perimeter signals that your home is prepared and not worth the effort.

Unlike interior fortifications, which focus on protecting specific entry points like doors and windows, perimeter defenses aim to keep threats at a distance. By setting up physical and psychological barriers, you make it more difficult for intruders to even approach your home, much less break into it.

The best perimeter defenses are layered. This means creating multiple levels of protection that work together to slow down or stop intruders at various points along the perimeter. From fences to surveillance systems to landscaping choices, each element plays a part in creating a secure boundary around your property.

Erecting Physical Barriers

One of the most straightforward ways to build a perimeter defense is by erecting physical barriers. These barriers can be fences, walls, or gates, designed to prevent easy access to your property. However, it's important to recognize that not all barriers are created equal. The right choice for your home will depend on the layout of your property, your budget, and the level of security you're aiming for.

A fence is the most common form of perimeter defense. While traditional wood fences provide privacy, they may not be the most secure option unless reinforced. Chain-link fences offer visibility, making it harder for intruders to approach undetected, but they can also be climbed unless they're topped with barbed wire or spikes. For those seeking a middle ground, wrought iron fences combine durability with aesthetic appeal and can be customized to include anti-climb features.

If a fence isn't practical or desirable, natural barriers can be just as effective. Thorny bushes or hedges like Hawthorn, Holly, or Pyracantha are excellent choices for creating a natural fence that's both attractive and difficult to penetrate. Planting these dense, thorny shrubs along your property line makes it uncomfortable and dangerous for intruders to attempt entry. Additionally, these plants don't require much maintenance and can blend seamlessly into your landscaping.

For properties with larger areas to secure, gates are another key feature. Driveway gates not only provide an additional layer of security but also limit access to vehicles. Opt for automatic gates that can be controlled remotely, allowing you to manage access without needing to leave the safety of your home. Strong metal gates, especially those with integrated locking mechanisms, are far more secure than wooden gates or simple latches.

Adding Visual Deterrents

While physical barriers are effective, sometimes the mere perception of security is enough to stop an intruder in their tracks. Visual deterrents like signs, lights, and surveillance cameras play a crucial role in building a perimeter defense. Even if an intruder isn't physically stopped by a fence, they might think twice if they see signs indicating a robust security system.

One of the simplest and most affordable ways to deter intruders is by installing motion-activated floodlights around your property. Intruders prefer to operate under the cover of darkness, and sudden, bright lights will often scare them off before they even attempt to break in. These lights are easy to install and can be placed along fences, gates, or near entry points to ensure that anyone approaching is immediately illuminated.

Surveillance cameras are another powerful visual deterrent. Even if you don't have a full surveillance system installed, just the sight of a camera can be enough to make intruders think twice. Place cameras at key points around your perimeter — near gates, along driveways, and at entry points — to maximize visibility. Some homeowners opt for a mix of real and dummy cameras, which are inexpensive and still serve as effective deterrents. However, for full coverage and peace of mind, invest in a system that allows you to monitor activity in real-time.

Using Landscaping as Defense

Landscaping plays a surprisingly large role in perimeter defense. How you design and maintain your yard can either invite or deter intruders. The goal is to create a landscape that not only looks good but also makes it difficult for anyone to approach your home unnoticed or unhindered.

As mentioned earlier, thorny bushes and dense shrubs make excellent natural barriers. But beyond that, consider the layout of your yard. Keep trees and tall bushes away from windows, as they can provide cover for someone trying to break in. Trim back overgrown areas that could obscure sightlines, especially around entry points.

In addition to using plants as barriers, gravel walkways or driveways can add an extra layer of security. The sound of crunching gravel is hard to avoid, making it nearly impossible for someone to approach your home quietly. This can serve as an early alert system, giving you time to assess the situation and respond accordingly.

Integrating Technology into Perimeter Defense

The final layer of your perimeter defense involves integrating technology to monitor and secure your property. Modern surveillance and monitoring systems provide a wealth of options that can enhance your overall security.

Motion sensors placed at strategic points along the perimeter can alert you to any movement, sending real-time notifications to your phone or security system. These sensors are ideal for areas that might be more difficult to monitor visually, such as long driveways or large backyards. When paired with cameras, they provide a comprehensive solution that ensures every inch of your perimeter is being watched.

Another powerful tool is the use of electric fencing. While more expensive and often reserved for high-security areas, electric fencing is incredibly effective at deterring intruders. If you opt for this, ensure it complies with local regulations and is installed by a professional to avoid any accidental harm to yourself or family members.

CHAPTER 2

ENERGY INDEPENDENCE AND OFF-GRID SOLUTIONS

Assessing Your Household's Energy Needs

Achieving energy independence is a key component of being prepared for any crisis, and the first step toward reaching this goal is to accurately assess your household's energy needs. Whether you're looking to go completely off-grid or simply want to ensure you have reliable backup power during an emergency, understanding how much energy your household consumes and where you can cut back is essential. This chapter will guide you through the process of evaluating your current energy usage, identifying critical energy needs, and finding areas where you can improve efficiency. For someone like Jack, who values self-reliance and has a clear focus on practical solutions, this assessment is not only about survival but about creating a sustainable, independent household.

The importance of knowing your energy needs cannot be overstated, especially when planning for off-grid solutions or long-term emergencies. In a crisis, your ability to manage energy consumption effectively can make all the difference. By understanding your baseline energy usage, you'll be able to prioritize which systems need power the most, identify where you can make cuts, and plan accordingly for backup solutions like solar panels or generators. The key is not just to meet your energy needs but to do so efficiently and sustainably.

Understanding Baseline Energy Usage

The first step in assessing your household's energy needs is understanding your baseline energy usage. This involves calculating how much energy your household consumes on a daily and monthly basis. Most utility companies provide detailed energy usage reports, but you can also calculate this manually by reviewing your electric bill and noting the kilowatt-hours (kWh) consumed each month.

Once you have a clear picture of your average monthly usage, it's time to break that number down into categories. Ask yourself: *Which appliances and systems are consuming the most power?* Typically, heating and cooling systems, refrigerators, and other large appliances are the primary energy consumers in most homes. Understanding which appliances are using the most energy will help you prioritize where to focus your efforts.

Start by identifying the non-negotiable systems — those that you absolutely cannot go without during a crisis. For example, heating or cooling may be critical depending on the climate you live in. Additionally, refrigerators and freezers are necessary to keep food from spoiling, and any medical devices that require power must also be accounted for. Make a list of these essential systems and note how much energy each one requires on a daily basis.

Beyond essential systems, consider the comfort and convenience appliances that may not be critical to survival but would greatly improve your quality of life during a prolonged power outage. These might include lights, cooking appliances, or entertainment devices like TVs and radios. While these may not be your top priority, it's worth noting how much energy they consume and whether they can be powered with alternative sources like solar energy or battery backups.

Estimating Energy Needs in a Crisis

During a crisis, your energy consumption patterns will likely change, especially if you're relying on backup power sources like generators or solar panels. To prepare effectively, you'll need to estimate how much energy you would use in a worst-case scenario. For Jack, who is preparing his household to function independently during emergencies, it's crucial to understand how to adapt energy usage to conserve fuel and resources.

Start by revisiting your list of essential systems and appliances. In a crisis, you won't be running everything as you would during normal times, so it's important to calculate how much energy these essential systems will require over a 24-hour period. For example, if you rely on a refrigerator to keep food safe, calculate how many kWh it uses per hour and how many hours it typically runs each day. Similarly, if you need heating or cooling, determine how much energy your HVAC system consumes and whether there are more efficient alternatives available, such as space heaters or fans powered by generators.

Next, think about lighting. While lighting is often overlooked, it can account for a significant portion of energy consumption, especially during long-term outages. Consider switching to LED bulbs, which consume far less energy than traditional incandescent bulbs, and use motion-activated or timed lights to reduce unnecessary usage. Small changes in lighting can lead to substantial savings in energy.

It's also important to factor in energy needs for communication devices like cell phones, radios, and laptops. In a crisis, staying connected to news and emergency updates is crucial, so you'll need to ensure that these devices can remain charged. Estimate the energy requirements for charging these devices and look into portable solar chargers or battery packs as efficient solutions to meet this need.

Prioritizing Energy for Critical Systems

Once you've calculated your energy needs during a crisis, it's time to prioritize. The reality is, when running on limited power sources like generators or solar panels, you won't be able to power every system and appliance in your home at full capacity. This is where prioritizing your energy needs becomes critical.

Rank your essential systems based on importance, starting with those that are absolutely necessary for survival, such as heating, refrigeration, and medical devices. These systems should receive the bulk of your backup power resources. Then, move on to comfort and convenience appliances, deciding which ones are worth powering during an extended outage. While it might be nice to run a TV or charge a laptop, these items should be lower on the priority list than critical systems.

For each system, think about ways to minimize energy consumption. For example, you can reduce the energy used by a refrigerator by keeping it fully stocked (since a full refrigerator uses less energy to stay cold) and minimizing how often you open the door. If heating is a priority, consider insulating your home to retain as much heat as possible, reducing the need for constant heating. These small adjustments can help stretch your energy resources during a crisis.

Planning for Future Energy Efficiency

After assessing your household's current energy needs and understanding what would be required in a crisis, it's time to start thinking about future efficiency. Even if you're not ready to go completely off-grid, there are many ways to reduce your overall energy consumption and make your home more energy-efficient, saving money and ensuring greater energy independence in the long run.

One of the most effective ways to improve energy efficiency is by upgrading appliances to energy-efficient models. Look for appliances with the Energy Star label, which indicates that they use significantly less power than standard models. While these upgrades can be costly upfront, they pay off in reduced energy bills and lower demands on backup power systems during emergencies.

Another key area to focus on is insulation and weatherproofing. Poor insulation can cause your home to lose heat in the winter and cool air in the summer, leading to higher energy consumption. Sealing gaps in doors and windows, adding insulation to walls and attics, and using weatherstripping can significantly reduce energy loss, making your home more efficient and less reliant on constant heating or cooling.

DIY Solar Power Solutions

In the pursuit of energy independence, one of the most effective and sustainable strategies you can adopt is harnessing the power of the sun. Solar power is a renewable, clean source of energy that can significantly reduce your reliance on traditional power grids, while providing you with a reliable source of electricity during crises or outages. For someone like Jack, who values hands-on solutions and long-term energy security, DIY solar power systems are an excellent way to fortify his home and ensure a continuous energy supply.

Installing solar power doesn't require an expensive contractor or high-tech systems. In fact, with a little research and careful planning, it's possible to design and implement a DIY solar setup that meets your household's energy needs without the overwhelming costs of professional installations. This section will walk you through the basics of solar power, the components you need, and practical steps to building a system that will keep your home powered through even the most challenging circumstances.

Understanding How Solar Power Works

Before diving into the installation process, it's essential to have a solid understanding of how solar power works. Solar power systems use photovoltaic (PV) panels to capture sunlight and convert it into usable electricity. These panels are made up of many small cells that absorb sunlight and release electrons, creating an electric current. The energy generated by these cells is then passed through an inverter, which converts the direct current (DC) produced by the panels into alternating current (AC), the type of electricity used to power most household appliances.

In a DIY setup, the solar panels collect energy during the day, and this energy is stored in batteries or used immediately to power your home. The key to a successful solar system is ensuring that the number of panels and the storage capacity are sufficient to meet your energy needs, especially during extended periods without access to traditional grid power.

Choosing the Right Solar Panels

When it comes to building your DIY solar power solution, one of the most important decisions is choosing the right solar panels. There are several types of solar panels available, and each has its own advantages depending on your energy needs, budget, and space availability.

For homeowners like Jack, monocrystalline panels are often the best option. These panels are made from pure silicon and are known for their high efficiency and durability. Monocrystalline panels are especially useful if you have limited roof space, as they generate more electricity per square foot than other types of panels. While they tend to be more expensive upfront, their long lifespan and efficiency make them a worthwhile investment in the long run.

Another option is polycrystalline panels, which are more affordable but slightly less efficient than monocrystalline panels. They are a good choice if you have more space available and are looking to save on initial costs. Thin-film panels are the least efficient but also the cheapest and lightest, making them an option for smaller or temporary solar setups.

When selecting panels, also consider the wattage — the amount of power each panel can generate. Higher wattage panels can generate more energy, but they also tend to be larger and more expensive. If you're working with limited space or budget, you might opt for lower wattage panels and compensate by installing more of them.

Building Your Solar Power System

Once you've selected your panels, it's time to start building your solar power system. For a basic DIY setup, you'll need a few key components beyond just the panels:

- **Inverter:** Converts the DC power generated by the panels into AC power that your home can use. Inverters come in different sizes, so be sure to choose one that matches the total output of your solar array.
- **Charge Controller:** Regulates the flow of electricity from the solar panels to the batteries, preventing overcharging and ensuring a steady supply of power.
- **Batteries:** Store the energy generated by your panels for use during the night or on cloudy days. Deep-cycle batteries, such as those used in off-grid setups, are ideal for solar systems because they can be discharged and recharged repeatedly.
- **Mounting Hardware:** The racks or brackets used to secure your panels to your roof or another surface.

Start by determining where your solar panels will be mounted. The best location is usually a south-facing roof that gets plenty of direct sunlight throughout the day. If your roof isn't suitable, ground-mounted panels are an alternative, though they require more space and additional installation steps. Make sure to avoid areas that are shaded by trees or buildings, as even a small amount of shade can significantly reduce the efficiency of your panels.

Once the panels are mounted, connect them to the inverter and charge controller, which will regulate the flow of energy to your battery bank. The size of your battery bank will depend on how much energy you need to store, but a good rule of thumb is to have enough capacity to power your essential systems for at least 24 hours. For larger homes, this might mean investing in multiple batteries.

Expanding Your System Over Time

One of the great advantages of a DIY solar power system is its flexibility. Unlike a traditional grid-tied system, which is often installed all at once by professionals, a DIY solar setup can be expanded over time. Start by installing enough panels and batteries to meet your essential energy needs, such as powering lights, refrigerators, and communication devices during an outage.

Once your basic system is up and running, you can gradually add more panels or increase your battery storage to power additional appliances or systems. This modular approach allows you to build your energy independence gradually, without needing to make a massive financial investment upfront.

In addition to expanding the number of panels, you can also look into integrating portable solar solutions into your setup. Portable solar generators or foldable panels can be used to charge smaller devices, run power tools, or even provide energy when you're away from home. These smaller, flexible options are an excellent addition for someone like Jack, who enjoys hands-on projects and values the ability to adapt to different situations.

Reducing Energy Consumption for Greater Efficiency

To maximize the effectiveness of your DIY solar power system, it's crucial to reduce your overall energy consumption. The less energy your home requires, the more of it you can supply through solar power alone. Simple adjustments like switching to LED light bulbs, using energy-efficient appliances, and implementing smart home devices that control when and how much energy is used can significantly reduce the load on your solar system.

Energy conservation is especially important during periods of low sunlight or when battery capacity is limited. In these situations, focus on powering only the essential systems, such as refrigerators, medical devices, or heating and cooling systems, while cutting back on non-essential appliances like televisions or power-hungry kitchen gadgets.

Backup Generators and Alternatives

When preparing for long-term energy independence, backup generators are one of the most crucial components to consider. While solar power systems can provide a sustainable and renewable source of energy, there will be times — especially during prolonged periods of low sunlight or emergencies — when you'll need an alternative solution to keep your household running. For Jack, a homeowner focused on being prepared for any crisis, having a reliable backup power source ensures that his family remains safe and comfortable even during extended outages.

This section explores the different types of backup generators available, how they fit into a comprehensive energy strategy, and alternative solutions that can complement or even replace traditional generators in some scenarios. Whether you're looking for a permanent backup system or something more flexible and portable, understanding your options will help you make the right choice for your specific energy needs.

Types of Backup Generators

When it comes to backup generators, there are two main types that homeowners generally consider: portable generators and standby generators. Both have their advantages, and the choice depends largely on your energy needs, budget, and how much power you need to generate during an outage.

Portable generators are smaller, more affordable, and can be moved from one location to another. They are usually powered by gasoline or propane and can supply enough electricity to power essential appliances like refrigerators, lights, and communication devices. Because they are portable, they offer flexibility and can be used in various situations, including camping trips or providing temporary power to other locations. However, they have limitations, particularly in terms of how much power they can generate. Portable generators are typically best suited for short-term outages or as a secondary backup system to a larger, more permanent setup.

On the other hand, standby generators are larger, fixed systems that automatically turn on when they detect a power outage. These generators are typically powered by natural gas, propane, or diesel and are connected directly to your home's electrical system. Standby generators can provide enough power to run your entire household, including heating and cooling systems, and can operate for days or even weeks as long as they are properly fueled. The main advantage of standby generators is their ability to provide uninterrupted power without any manual intervention, making them ideal for long-term outages or situations where consistent energy is critical. However, they are more expensive to install and maintain compared to portable options.

For Jack, who values practicality and flexibility, a hybrid approach may be the best solution. By combining a portable generator for quick, short-term needs with a standby generator for longer outages, he ensures that his family has a reliable power source in any situation.

Choosing the Right Fuel Source

One of the key considerations when selecting a backup generator is the type of fuel it uses. Each fuel source has its advantages and disadvantages, depending on your location, budget, and energy needs.

*   Gasoline is one of the most common fuels for portable generators. It's readily available, but it has a limited shelf life, making it less ideal for long-term storage. Gasoline generators are typically less expensive upfront but require careful fuel management, especially during extended outages. For short-term solutions, gasoline is a convenient and effective fuel, but for Jack's long-term crisis preparation, it might not be the best option.

*   Propane is a popular alternative to gasoline because it has a longer shelf life and burns cleaner, making it a more environmentally friendly option. Propane generators are often dual-fuel, meaning they can also run on gasoline if needed. The downside to propane is that it requires more storage space, as it must be kept in large tanks. However, for homeowners with space and the ability to store propane safely, it's an excellent choice for powering both portable and standby generators.

*   Natural gas is another common fuel for standby generators. It's convenient because it's connected directly to your home's existing gas line, ensuring a constant fuel supply as long as the natural gas network remains operational. This eliminates the need for fuel storage and reduces the risk of running out of power. However, in some crisis situations, such as earthquakes or gas line disruptions, natural gas may not be avail-

able. For those living in areas with reliable natural gas infrastructure, this is often the most hassle-free fuel option.

- Diesel is often used in larger standby generators because it's efficient and provides more power per gallon than gasoline or propane. Diesel generators are highly reliable and can run for long periods without needing a refill. However, like gasoline, diesel has a limited shelf life and can be difficult to store for long periods. Diesel generators are commonly used in commercial and industrial settings but can also be a powerful option for homeowners looking for a robust, long-lasting power source.

Solar-Powered Generators

While traditional generators rely on fossil fuels, solar-powered generators offer a cleaner, renewable alternative that can be integrated into your energy strategy. Solar generators work by collecting sunlight through solar panels and converting it into electricity, which is stored in batteries for later use. These systems are ideal for homeowners who already have solar panels installed, as they can provide backup power without relying on fuel supplies.

Solar generators are typically smaller and less powerful than traditional generators, making them better suited for charging devices, powering lights, or running small appliances. However, with advances in battery technology, some solar-powered generators can now provide enough power to run larger systems, like refrigerators or medical devices, for extended periods. The key advantage of solar generators is that they don't require fuel, making them an excellent solution for long-term crises where fuel supplies may be limited or unavailable.

For Jack, who is focused on creating a sustainable and renewable energy system, a solar-powered generator could complement his existing setup. While it may not provide as much power as a gasoline or propane generator, it offers a reliable backup option for smaller energy needs.

Alternatives to Backup Generators

While backup generators are the most common solution for power outages, there are other alternatives that can help you maintain energy independence without relying solely on fuel-based systems. One option is to invest in a battery backup system, which stores electricity generated by solar panels or the grid when power is available and releases it during outages.

Battery systems, like the Tesla Powerwall or other deep-cycle batteries, are becoming increasingly popular as they offer silent, low-maintenance energy storage solutions. Unlike traditional generators, they don't require fuel, and once installed, they operate automatically, switching on when grid power fails. Battery backups are ideal for homeowners who already have solar panels installed and want a quiet, emissions-free alternative to generators. However, they do have limitations in terms of how much energy they can store, making them less suitable for long-term outages unless paired with other systems.

Another alternative is using wind turbines. While less common in residential settings, small wind turbines can be installed on properties with enough open space to generate electricity. Like solar power, wind turbines are renewable and don't require fuel, but they are more location-dependent, requiring consistent wind speeds to generate sufficient energy.

Energy Conservation During Crises

When disaster strikes and energy becomes a scarce resource, the ability to conserve energy is critical to sustaining your household's needs. Whether you're relying on a back-up generator, solar panels, or stored fuel, making sure that your energy lasts as long as possible is a top priority. During crises, when there is uncertainty about how long power outages or shortages will last, understanding how to efficiently manage and reduce your energy consumption can make all the difference. For Jack, a buyer persona focused on being prepared for any situation, this chapter will provide practical strategies to maximize energy conservation and ensure that his family can survive extended periods with limited resources.

Energy conservation isn't just about cutting back on comfort; it's about smart planning, resource management, and creating systems that allow your household to function with minimal energy use. In the following sections, we'll explore how to prioritize essential energy needs, make use of energy-efficient solutions, and implement practical techniques to stretch your energy reserves during times of crisis.

Prioritizing Essential Energy Needs

In any crisis, the first step in conserving energy is identifying which systems and appliances are non-negotiable and must remain operational. This means focusing on the essentials that keep your household functioning and safe. Heating and cooling, lighting, communication devices, and medical equipment are some of the critical systems that often take priority during energy shortages.

For Jack, it's important to establish a hierarchy of energy needs. Begin by identifying the systems that are necessary for survival. If you live in a cold climate, keeping your home heated is crucial. In hot climates, cooling systems or fans may be necessary to prevent overheating. Likewise, refrigerators and freezers are essential for keeping food from spoiling, while communication devices like cell phones and radios are necessary to stay informed during a disaster.

Once you've determined which systems are essential, calculate how much energy each one consumes and determine how you can minimize that usage. For example, refrigerators don't need to be opened frequently during an outage. Keep them sealed as much as possible to conserve the cold inside, which reduces the amount of time the compressor has to run. Similarly, space heaters or fans should be used strategically — only heating or cooling the rooms your family is using at the time, rather than the entire house.

Implementing Energy-Efficient Solutions

While prioritizing energy needs is important, it's equally crucial to find energy-efficient alternatives to your everyday appliances. One of the simplest and most effective ways to reduce energy consumption is by replacing older, power-hungry devices with more efficient models. For example, LED light bulbs consume far less electricity than traditional incandescent bulbs and last much longer. Switching to LEDs is a quick and inexpensive way to cut down on energy use during a crisis, ensuring that your backup power system lasts longer.

Another highly effective method for conserving energy is using smart power strips. Many appliances, even when turned off, continue to draw power in the form of "phantom loads." A smart power strip automatically cuts off power to devices that are not in use, saving you valuable energy. During a crisis, you'll want to minimize any unnecessary energy drain, and power strips are a convenient solution for managing multiple appliances with ease.

Beyond swapping out appliances, consider investing in solar-powered gadgets that require no external electricity. Solar lanterns, battery chargers, and radios can all function off-grid and can be recharged during the day, giving you more flexibility in how you use your energy. These tools are particularly useful in times of extended outages or when fuel supplies are limited.

Reducing Energy Usage in Daily Activities

During a crisis, it's not enough to simply rely on energy-efficient appliances and systems — you also need to make deliberate efforts to reduce your daily energy consumption. Small changes in how you use energy can add up, extending the life of your power supply and ensuring that you have enough for essential functions.

One of the most effective strategies is timing your energy use. For example, many households use most of their energy in the evenings when the entire family is home. However, during a crisis, you can spread out your energy usage throughout the day to prevent overloading your system. Use the daylight hours to perform tasks that don't require much electricity, like cooking or cleaning. When night falls, limit the use of lights and appliances to only what is absolutely necessary.

Another way to reduce energy consumption is by batching tasks. Instead of using your oven or stove multiple times a day, prepare meals in one cooking session. Likewise, run devices like washing machines or dishwashers only when you have a full load, rather than multiple smaller loads. Batching tasks minimizes the frequency of energy-intensive activities and reduces the overall consumption of power.

To conserve fuel, avoid using power-hungry appliances like air conditioners, electric stoves, or dryers if possible. Instead, consider alternative methods that require little to no energy, such as air-drying clothes or using a wood stove for heating and cooking. These simple lifestyle changes can make a significant difference when power is in short supply.

Insulating and Weatherproofing Your Home

One of the most overlooked yet critical aspects of energy conservation is insulating and weatherproofing your home. A well-insulated home will retain heat in the winter and stay cooler in the summer, reducing the amount of energy required for heating and cooling. This is especially important during crises when fuel and electricity are scarce.

Start by sealing windows and doors to prevent drafts. Even a small gap around a window frame can let in cold air, forcing your heating system to work harder. Apply weatherstripping around doors and caulk around windows to ensure that your home stays as airtight as possible. For extra insulation, you can also install thermal curtains or use blankets to cover drafty windows and doorways.

In the winter months, focus on insulating key areas of your home, such as attics, basements, and crawl spaces, which are common sources of heat loss. If insulating the entire home isn't feasible, try to create a smaller, well-insulated zone within the house where your family can spend most of their time. This "warm zone" can be heated more efficiently, while the rest of the house remains unheated.

Leveraging Natural Light and Ventilation

In addition to weatherproofing your home, make use of natural light and ventilation to reduce your reliance on artificial lighting and air conditioning. During the day, open blinds or curtains to allow sunlight to illuminate your home, reducing the need for electric lights. On sunny days, the heat from the sun can also help warm your home, reducing the need for heaters.

In warmer climates, take advantage of natural ventilation by opening windows during cooler parts of the day, like early morning or evening, to let in fresh air. Use fans sparingly and only when necessary. Proper airflow can help regulate your home's temperature without relying on energy-hungry air conditioning units.

Ensuring Fuel Safety and Conservation

During crises or extended periods off-grid, fuel becomes a precious resource that must be carefully managed. Whether you rely on propane, gasoline, diesel, or natural gas to power generators, heaters, or vehicles, ensuring that your fuel is both stored safely and used efficiently is critical to maintaining your household's energy independence. For Jack, who values self-sufficiency and preparedness, knowing how to store and conserve fuel will provide peace of mind and help ensure that his family can weather any emergency without running out of critical resources.

This section will guide you through the best practices for storing fuel safely, managing fuel consumption, and making the most of every drop during an extended crisis.

Storing Fuel Safely

One of the primary concerns when dealing with fuel storage is safety. Many types of fuel, such as gasoline and propane, are highly flammable and require proper handling to prevent accidents. Storing fuel incorrectly can lead to fires, leaks, and even health hazards. That's why it's crucial to take the necessary precautions to ensure your fuel storage is secure and safe for long-term use.

CHOOSING THE RIGHT CONTAINERS

The first step in safe fuel storage is choosing the right containers. Each type of fuel has specific requirements when it comes to containers, and using the wrong type can lead to dangerous leaks or contamination. Gasoline should be stored in approved containers made of metal or high-density polyethylene plastic that are specifically designed for gasoline storage. These containers should have secure, childproof caps and be labeled clearly to avoid confusion.

Propane, on the other hand, is stored in cylinders or tanks that are pressure-rated for propane storage. It's important to check that the tanks you use are certified for safety and are not damaged or corroded. Diesel fuel, similar to gasoline, can be stored in containers designed for diesel, which are often color-coded (yellow) to differentiate them from gasoline (red).

Keep in mind that fuel containers should never be filled beyond 95% capacity, as fuel expands and contracts with temperature changes. Overfilling containers can cause spills, leaks, or even explosions if the fuel has nowhere to expand.

SELECTING A STORAGE LOCATION

Once you've chosen the proper containers, the next step is selecting a safe storage location. Fuel should always be stored in a cool, dry, and well-ventilated area. This helps prevent the buildup of fumes, which could lead to fire hazards. Avoid storing fuel inside your home or garage if possible. Instead, opt for a dedicated storage shed or outdoor area that is well away from living spaces.

For propane and gasoline, avoid direct sunlight or areas where temperatures fluctuate dramatically, as heat can increase the pressure in containers and cause them to rupture. If you live in a hot climate, consider creating a shaded or insulated area for fuel storage to minimize temperature-related risks.

ROTATING FUEL STOCKS

Fuel has a limited shelf life, and storing it for too long without proper care can lead to degradation, contamination, or even total unusability. Gasoline, for instance, can begin to degrade in as little as three months unless treated with a fuel stabilizer. Stabilizers extend the life of fuel by preventing oxidation and the formation of harmful deposits.

The key to managing long-term fuel storage is rotating your fuel stocks. This means using the oldest fuel first and replenishing your supply with fresh fuel as you go. A good practice is to label each container with the date it was filled, making it easier to track which fuel to use first.

For Jack, this approach ensures that fuel is always fresh and ready for use in a crisis, minimizing the risk of being stuck with unusable fuel when it's needed the most. By following a rotation schedule and incorporating stabilizers, stored fuel can last up to 12 to 24 months, depending on the type and storage conditions.

Conserving Fuel During a Crisis

Fuel is often in short supply during emergencies, especially if fuel stations are out of service or deliveries are delayed. This makes fuel conservation a top priority, as every drop counts when you don't know how long the crisis will last. Being strategic about how you use fuel can significantly extend your supply and help you maintain essential services for as long as possible.

PRIORITIZING FUEL USE

Just as with energy conservation, prioritizing essential systems is crucial when it comes to fuel usage. Identify which systems and devices are critical to your household's survival — such as generators, heating systems, and vehicles — and allocate fuel accordingly. Avoid wasting fuel on non-essential appliances or activities, especially if you're uncertain about how long your fuel supply needs to last.

For example, if Jack's generator is running low on fuel, he might choose to power only the essentials, like the refrigerator and medical devices, while turning off non-essential systems such as entertainment devices. In this scenario, keeping the generator running only at peak times or for a few hours per day could extend the fuel supply for days or even weeks.

USING FUEL-EFFICIENT DEVICES

Another key strategy in fuel conservation is using fuel-efficient devices. When it comes to generators, for instance, models with inverter technology are typically more fuel-efficient than conventional generators. Inverter generators adjust their power output to match the energy load, using less fuel when demand is lower. If Jack is planning to invest in a backup generator, opting for an energy-efficient model will ensure that he gets the most power for the least amount of fuel.

Likewise, if you're using fuel for heating, consider fuel-efficient heaters such as propane space heaters, which can heat a room quickly and with less fuel than a traditional furnace.

Carpooling and Limiting Vehicle Use

Fuel is also a critical resource for transportation, and during a crisis, access to gasoline or diesel may be limited. One way to conserve fuel in vehicles is by reducing unnecessary trips, carpooling, or using bicycles or other non-fuel-based transportation methods when possible.

If Jack and his family need to travel, planning trips carefully to minimize fuel consumption — such as combining errands into a single outing — can help reduce fuel usage. If neighbors are in a similar situation, organizing a carpool for necessary trips can further reduce fuel consumption and help the entire community manage their resources more effectively.

Securing Fuel During a Crisis

In addition to conserving fuel, it's important to know how to secure your fuel during a crisis. Fuel theft can become a serious issue during emergencies when supplies are limited, and desperate individuals may resort to stealing fuel from storage containers or vehicles. To protect your fuel supply, consider investing in locking fuel caps for your gas containers and vehicles, as well as using secure storage sheds with padlocks or other security measures.

For larger fuel supplies, fencing off the storage area or using motion-activated lighting or alarms can deter potential thieves. Additionally, keeping fuel storage areas out of sight from passersby reduces the likelihood that your fuel will become a target.

CHAPTER 3
WATER STORAGE AND PURIFICATION

- -

Understanding Your Home's Water Needs

Water is a fundamental resource for survival, and understanding your home's water needs is the first step in ensuring that your household remains well-supplied during any crisis. Whether you are planning for a short-term emergency or preparing for long-term off-grid living, knowing how much water your family requires is crucial to maintaining health and hygiene in challenging situations. For Jack, who values self-reliance and wants to ensure his family is ready for anything, calculating and preparing for water needs is just as important as energy independence or food storage.

When planning for water storage and usage, it's essential to consider not only the immediate drinking needs but also the water required for hygiene, cooking, and even gardening if you plan to grow food. Each person and household will have different requirements based on lifestyle, climate, and specific needs, but there are general guidelines and strategies that can help you estimate your water usage and prepare accordingly.

Calculating Daily Water Needs

The average person needs around one gallon of water per day for basic survival, which includes both drinking and minimal hygiene. However, this number can vary depending on individual health, climate, and physical activity levels. In hotter climates, where dehydration becomes a greater risk, or for individuals engaged in strenuous activities, daily water needs can easily double.

For a family like Jack's, it's important to plan for a minimum of one gallon per person per day just for drinking water, but it's wise to account for a more realistic usage scenario by including hygiene and other needs. For basic hygiene, such as washing hands, face, and brushing teeth, an additional half gallon per person per day is typically sufficient. This brings the total recommended daily water usage to approximately 1.5 gallons per person.

It's also important to consider cooking water. Many emergency food supplies, such as dehydrated meals or grains, require water for preparation. Depending on the type of food stored and the cooking methods used, you may need to allocate half a gallon of water per day for cooking per household member.

For a family of four, this translates into about 6 to 8 gallons of water per day, assuming moderate usage. However, Jack, who is focused on thorough preparedness, might want to add a buffer to this estimate. Planning for 2 to 3 gallons per person will give your household a comfortable margin of error, particularly in extreme climates or during physically demanding tasks like building, fortifying, or gardening.

Factoring in Hygiene and Sanitation

While the drinking and cooking needs are straightforward, hygiene and sanitation account for a significant portion of water usage in daily life, even during emergencies. One of the biggest challenges during a crisis, especially in long-term off-grid scenarios, is managing water for sanitation purposes. Flushing toilets, showering, and even laundry can consume a surprising amount of water if not carefully managed.

A standard toilet uses about 1.6 gallons per flush, so if water is scarce, you'll want to adopt a "if it's yellow, let it mellow" approach, flushing only when absolutely necessary. Alternatively, composting toilets or portable chemical toilets can be a water-saving solution in off-grid or emergency situations.

Bathing and laundry are two other areas where water usage can quickly spiral out of control. In a crisis, especially if clean water is limited, prioritizing sponge baths or quick rinses rather than full showers is essential. If your household normally consumes large amounts of water for these tasks, start practicing conservation techniques like reusing greywater (water from washing dishes or bathing) for flushing toilets or watering plants.

Greywater systems can be simple to set up and are an excellent way to make the most out of the water you have stored. Capturing water from handwashing or dishwashing and repurposing it can drastically reduce how much water your household consumes, particularly in longer-term crises.

Special Considerations for Children, Elderly, and Pets

When calculating your home's water needs, it's important to account for any special requirements that may exist within your household. Children and elderly family members are more vulnerable to dehydration, especially in extreme temperatures, and may require additional water for drinking. Children, in particular, can be more active and therefore need more hydration, while elderly individuals may have medical conditions that necessitate more frequent hydration or specific water requirements for medications.

Pets are another factor that can be easily overlooked when planning for water storage. Dogs, cats, and other household pets have daily water needs just like humans, and it's important to ensure that they are accounted for in your overall water plan. A medium-sized dog typically drinks about half a gallon of water per day, while cats require closer to one cup. Be sure to include their water requirements in your overall calculations to avoid running out during an emergency.

Planning for Long-Term Water Needs

While short-term crises may only require enough water to last a few days to a week, long-term emergencies pose a different challenge entirely. For extended off-grid living or disasters where water supplies may be disrupted for weeks or months, it's essential to plan for long-term water storage solutions that go beyond the initial stockpile.

For Jack, who prioritizes being prepared for any situation, long-term water needs mean having a system in place for renewable water sources. One of the best ways to ensure a consistent supply of water is through a rainwater harvesting system. This method involves capturing and storing rainwater, which can be filtered and purified for safe consumption. This kind of system can provide an ongoing water source that's independent of traditional infrastructure, making it ideal for off-grid scenarios.

Another option is identifying local water sources, such as nearby lakes, rivers, or streams. However, water from these sources must be carefully treated and filtered before use, as they can contain harmful pathogens or contaminants. Having the knowledge and tools to purify water is key in these situations, but more on that will be covered in a later chapter on purification techniques.

Estimating Crisis Duration and Stockpiling Water

When it comes to planning for water needs during an emergency, it's also important to think about the potential duration of the crisis. A short-term disaster may only require a few days' worth of water, while a long-term emergency could demand months of stored water. For Jack, stockpiling enough water for at least two weeks is a good starting point, with plans to extend that supply through renewable sources like rainwater harvesting or filtration from local water bodies.

Stockpiling water can be done by purchasing commercially bottled water, which has a long shelf life and is easily stored, or by filling large food-grade water containers for home storage. These containers come in various sizes, from 5-gallon jugs to 55-gallon barrels, and should be stored in a cool, dark place to prevent contamination.

DIY Rainwater Harvesting Systems

Water is an essential resource, and during a crisis, access to clean water can be limited or completely cut off. One of the most effective ways to ensure a continuous water supply, especially in an off-grid or emergency situation, is to set up a rainwater harvesting system. By capturing and storing rainwater, you can create a renewable source of water that helps sustain your household in the long term. For someone like Jack, who is dedicated to ensuring his family's preparedness, a DIY rainwater harvesting system is a practical and valuable addition to their home defense strategy.

Building a DIY rainwater harvesting system doesn't have to be complicated or expensive. With the right setup, you can collect thousands of gallons of water each year, which can be filtered and purified for drinking or used for non-potable purposes such as irrigation, cleaning, and sanitation. In this section, we'll explore how rainwater harvesting works, the components you'll need, and step-by-step instructions on how to create an efficient system tailored to your needs.

How Rainwater Harvesting Works

The basic principle behind rainwater harvesting is simple: you collect and store rainwater that falls on your roof or other surfaces. This water can then be used for a variety of purposes, including drinking, cooking, hygiene, and gardening. The key is to capture as much rainwater as possible and store it in a way that preserves its quality and ensures it's safe to use.

A rainwater harvesting system typically consists of three main components:

- **Collection:** Rainwater is collected from the roof via gutters and downspouts.
- **Filtration:** Debris, leaves, and other contaminants are filtered out before the water enters the storage tank.
- **Storage:** The water is stored in tanks or barrels until it's needed.

In climates where rainfall is abundant, a rainwater harvesting system can provide enough water to significantly reduce your reliance on municipal supplies or well water, making it a vital asset in times of crisis.

Components of a DIY Rainwater Harvesting System

Before you start building your rainwater harvesting system, it's important to gather the necessary components. Most DIY systems are straightforward and can be installed with basic materials that are easy to find. The primary components you'll need include:

- **Catchment Area:** This is usually your roof, where rainwater will be collected. The larger your roof, the more water you can collect.
- **Gutters and Downspouts:** Gutters direct the rainwater from the roof to the downspouts, which carry the water to the filtration and storage systems. Ensure your gutters are clean and in good condition to avoid clogging.
- **First Flush Diverter:** This component prevents the first few gallons of rainwater, which may contain debris, dirt, and contaminants, from entering your storage system. The first flush diverter redirects this water away, ensuring that only clean water is stored.
- **Filtration System:** Before the water enters the storage tank, it needs to be filtered to

remove any remaining debris, leaves, or small particles. A mesh filter or screen can be installed at the top of the storage tank to catch any contaminants.

- **Storage Tank or Barrel:** This is where the collected rainwater will be stored. You can use rain barrels, IBC (Intermediate Bulk Containers), or larger cisterns depending on your needs and available space.
- **Overflow System:** In periods of heavy rainfall, your storage tank may fill up quickly. An overflow system will prevent excess water from spilling out uncontrollably by directing it safely away from your home or property.

Each of these components plays a crucial role in ensuring that your rainwater harvesting system functions efficiently and provides clean, usable water.

Setting Up the Rainwater Collection System

Now that you have the basic components, let's walk through the steps to set up your rainwater harvesting system.

1. Prepare the Catchment Area: Begin by inspecting your roof, as this will be your primary catchment area. Make sure it's clean and free of debris, dirt, and any toxic materials that could contaminate the water. Some roofing materials, like asphalt, may contain chemicals that could leach into the water, so it's important to be aware of the type of roof you have.

2. Install Gutters and Downspouts: If your home doesn't already have gutters, you'll need to install them to direct rainwater into your storage system. Make sure the gutters are properly sloped toward the downspouts to ensure smooth water flow. Downspouts should lead directly into your storage system or through a filtration device to remove debris.

3. Add a First Flush Diverter: The first flush diverter is a critical component that improves the quality of your stored water by directing the initial runoff away from your storage tank. This initial runoff typically contains dirt, dust, and other contaminants that have settled on your roof. Installing a diverter ensures that these pollutants are kept out of your water supply.

4. Set Up the Filtration System: Before rainwater enters your storage tank, it should pass through a filter to remove any remaining debris. This can be as simple as a mesh screen or a more complex filtration system, depending on the quality of water you want. For drinking water, additional filtration and purification methods will be necessary, but for non-potable uses, a basic filter may suffice.

5. Install the Storage Tank: Choose a storage tank or barrels based on the amount of water you want to store. For small-scale systems, rain barrels with a capacity of 50 to 100 gallons work well. For larger systems, you can install cisterns or IBC tanks that hold several hundred or even thousands of gallons. Position the tank in a shaded area to prevent algae growth and ensure it's elevated slightly to allow for gravity-fed water distribution.

6. Overflow Management: To handle heavy rainfall, install an overflow pipe that directs

excess water away from your foundation or garden. This prevents water from accumulating around your home and causing potential damage.

Using and Maintaining Your System

Once your DIY rainwater harvesting system is installed, proper maintenance is crucial to ensure that it continues to function effectively. Regularly clean your gutters and downspouts to prevent blockages, and check your filters for debris buildup. Additionally, inspect the first flush diverter periodically to make sure it's operating correctly.

For Jack, who prioritizes long-term survival and energy independence, maintaining the water system is essential, particularly during times of crisis. By keeping the system in good condition, his family can enjoy a steady supply of water for both drinking and non-drinking purposes.

Maximizing the Use of Collected Rainwater

Rainwater can be used for a wide variety of tasks around the home, reducing the strain on other water sources during a crisis. While it's common to use rainwater for irrigation and gardening, it can also be used for flushing toilets, washing clothes, and even drinking, provided it's filtered and purified correctly.

For drinking purposes, it's important to purify rainwater through methods like boiling, UV purification, or using a high-quality water filter. This will remove any bacteria, viruses, or chemical contaminants that may still be present after initial filtration.

In times of crisis, having a functioning rainwater harvesting system gives Jack the ability to conserve municipal or stored water supplies, reducing dependency on outside resources and making his home more self-sufficient.

Purification Techniques for Safe Drinking Water

In any survival or off-grid situation, access to clean, safe drinking water is paramount. Even if you've managed to store a large supply of water or have set up a DIY rainwater harvesting system, it's critical to ensure that this water is properly purified before consumption. Unfiltered or contaminated water can carry harmful bacteria, viruses, and parasites that can lead to severe illness. For Jack, who prioritizes his family's safety in every aspect of preparedness, mastering water purification techniques is non-negotiable.

There are several methods to purify water, ranging from simple techniques to advanced systems. In this chapter, we will explore different methods of water purification, how they work, and when to use each one, ensuring that you always have access to potable water, regardless of the situation.

Why Water Purification Is Essential

Before diving into the various techniques, it's important to understand why purification is essential. Even water that appears clean to the naked eye can harbor dangerous pathogens that cause illnesses like cholera, dysentery, or giardia. During a crisis, when medical resources may be limited, the last thing you want is a preventable illness from contaminated water. While rainwater is generally safer than other sources, it can still collect pollutants, debris, and microorganisms from the roof or catchment system. Local water sources like lakes, rivers, and streams, though abundant, are often contaminated with organic and chemical waste.

Knowing how to purify water ensures that you and your family can stay hydrated without compromising your health.

Boiling Water

One of the oldest and most reliable water purification methods is boiling. Boiling water kills a wide range of pathogens, including bacteria, viruses, and parasites, making it an effective technique in almost any situation.

To purify water through boiling, follow these steps:

- Bring the water to a rolling boil for at least one minute (or three minutes if you are at higher altitudes). This ensures that harmful microorganisms are killed.
- Allow the water to cool before drinking.

Boiling is a great option if you have access to a heat source, such as a stove, fire, or propane burner. It's particularly useful for small quantities of water and works well if you need immediate, short-term purification. However, boiling does not remove chemical contaminants like heavy metals or pesticides, so it's best used with water sources that are known to be free from such pollutants, or after filtration.

Filtration Systems

Filtration is another essential technique for purifying water, especially when dealing with water that contains visible debris, dirt, or sediment. Filters work by passing water through a physical barrier that traps particles, bacteria, and protozoa. There are different types of filtration systems available, ranging from portable water filters to more advanced home filtration systems.

- **Portable water filters:** These are small, handheld devices that are perfect for emergencies, camping, or travel. They typically use a ceramic filter or hollow-fiber membrane to remove bacteria and protozoa. Many of these filters also include an activated carbon component, which helps remove odors and some chemical contaminants.
- **Gravity-fed water filters:** These are larger systems that rely on gravity to pull water through the filter. They're ideal for purifying larger quantities of water at home. One

popular example is the Berkey Water Filter, which can filter out bacteria, viruses, and chemicals, making it a favorite among preppers.

- **Pump filters:** These are useful in situations where you need to draw water from a low source, such as a shallow stream. By manually pumping water through the filter, you can remove harmful microorganisms.

While filtration alone may not eliminate viruses, it's highly effective in removing bacteria and protozoa, which are more common in natural water sources. To get the most comprehensive purification, filtration can be combined with other methods like boiling or chemical treatments.

Chemical Water Purification

In situations where you don't have access to a heat source or a filtration system, chemical water purification is an effective alternative. This method uses chemicals to kill bacteria, viruses, and protozoa, making water safe to drink. Two of the most common chemicals used for this purpose are chlorine and iodine.

- **Chlorine tablets:** These are lightweight and easy to store, making them a popular choice for emergency kits. To use, simply dissolve a chlorine tablet in your water, wait the recommended time (usually 30 minutes), and the water will be safe to drink.

- **Iodine tablets:** Similar to chlorine, iodine tablets are another chemical option for purifying water. Some people prefer iodine because it leaves less of a taste than chlorine, though it may not be suitable for long-term use as iodine can build up in the body over time.

It's important to note that chemical treatments are highly effective at killing microorganisms, but they do not remove debris or other contaminants. Therefore, it's a good idea to pre-filter the water through a cloth or mesh if it contains visible particles before adding the tablets.

UV Light Purification

A more advanced method of water purification is the use of UV light. UV purifiers work by exposing water to ultraviolet light, which destroys the DNA of microorganisms, rendering them unable to reproduce or cause infection. UV purifiers are fast, efficient, and capable of eliminating bacteria, viruses, and protozoa, making them an excellent option for households or individuals who want a quick, chemical-free solution.

- **Portable UV purifiers:** These are small devices, often resembling a pen, that you can carry in your emergency kit or backpack. To use, you simply stir the device in the water for the recommended time (usually around 90 seconds), and the water becomes safe to drink.

- **Home UV systems:** These are larger systems that can be installed at home and used to purify large quantities of water as it enters your plumbing system. They are ideal for purifying rainwater or well water.

While UV purification is highly effective, it has a few limitations. UV light cannot penetrate murky or cloudy water, so the water must first be filtered to remove any sediment. Additionally, UV devices require power to function, which could be a concern in an extended crisis where electricity is unavailable. However, many portable UV devices are battery-operated or solar-powered, providing flexibility in emergency situations.

Distillation

Distillation is a more complex water purification method but can be highly effective in situations where the water is heavily contaminated, particularly with chemicals, heavy metals, or salt (in the case of seawater). The distillation process involves boiling water and then capturing the steam as it condenses. This steam is free from contaminants, leaving behind impurities such as salts, metals, and pathogens.

To distill water, you need a heat source, a container to boil the water, and a system to collect the steam. Distillation is an excellent solution for creating pure drinking water from even the most contaminated sources, but it's time-consuming and requires a significant amount of energy, making it less practical for daily use unless it's absolutely necessary.

Storing Water for Short and Long-Term Crises

In times of crisis, access to clean, potable water can become scarce, making it essential to plan ahead and store enough water to cover both short-term emergencies and long-term survival scenarios. Water is the cornerstone of survival, and without a sufficient supply, even the most prepared household can quickly find itself in danger. For someone like Jack, who wants to ensure his family is ready for any eventuality, mastering water storage techniques is critical to maintaining health, hygiene, and peace of mind during an emergency.

In this section, we will explore the different approaches to water storage, how to calculate your household's needs for both short and long-term crises, and best practices for keeping your water supply safe and uncontaminated.

Short-Term Water Storage: Preparing for Immediate Emergencies

When preparing for short-term crises, such as natural disasters, power outages, or unexpected disruptions in municipal water supplies, you'll need to focus on storing enough water for a minimum of two weeks. Short-term water storage is generally easier to manage and can be achieved using containers that are easy to store and access.

The general rule of thumb is to store at least one gallon of water per person, per day, which covers basic drinking and minimal hygiene. For a family of four, this means storing 28 gallons of water to last two weeks. However, depending on your location and the specific emergency, you might need more if the crisis extends beyond two weeks or if the temperature is particularly high, increasing the need for hydration.

CONTAINERS FOR SHORT-TERM STORAGE

For short-term emergencies, commercially bottled water is often the most convenient and reliable option. Bottled water has a long shelf life and comes pre-packaged, ready for immediate use. Make sure to store it in a cool, dark place, and regularly rotate your supply to ensure it remains fresh.

If you prefer to store water yourself, use food-grade plastic containers, such as 5-gallon jugs or stackable water storage containers. These are designed to keep water safe from contamination and can be easily stored in closets, basements, or garages. When filling containers yourself, be sure to use clean, disinfected containers and fill them with tap water that has been treated with a small amount of unscented bleach (about 8 drops per gallon) to ensure it remains uncontaminated during storage.

Long-Term Water Storage: Planning for Extended Crises

In a long-term crisis, such as a severe natural disaster, social unrest, or widespread infrastructure failure, you'll need to prepare for months or even years without access to clean water. This requires a more robust water storage solution, as well as contingency plans for renewable water sources like rainwater harvesting or local water sources.

Long-term water storage requires a higher level of planning, as you'll need enough water to cover not just basic hydration but also hygiene, cooking, and possibly gardening if you're growing your own food.

For a family of four, planning for long-term crises might mean storing hundreds or even thousands of gallons of water. This water must be stored in large, durable containers that can keep the water safe for extended periods. In addition to stored water, it's important to have water purification systems in place to treat any water you might collect from alternative sources.

LARGE-SCALE WATER STORAGE SOLUTIONS

When planning for long-term water storage, larger containers such as 55-gallon barrels, water storage tanks, or even cisterns are ideal. These containers are made of heavy-duty, food-grade plastic that is designed to keep water safe for long periods. Here's how to use them effectively:

- **55-Gallon Barrels:** These are a popular option for long-term water storage and can be filled with tap water treated with bleach for disinfection. One barrel can provide enough water for a family of four for up to two weeks. Multiple barrels can be stored in a garage or basement and rotated as needed.
- **Intermediate Bulk Containers (IBCs):** For families with more space, IBCs are large,

cubic containers that can store up to 275 or 330 gallons of water. They are excellent for long-term storage and can be connected to rainwater harvesting systems for continuous water replenishment. IBCs should be stored in a shaded area to prevent algae growth and fitted with a filtration system to ensure the water remains potable.

- **Cisterns or Underground Tanks:** For those with larger properties, underground cisterns offer a discreet and efficient way to store massive quantities of water. These tanks can hold thousands of gallons and are often connected to rainwater or greywater systems. The main benefit of underground cisterns is their ability to keep water cool and protected from sunlight, reducing the risk of bacterial growth.

Maintaining Water Quality Over Time

One of the challenges of long-term water storage is ensuring that the water remains clean and safe to drink over months or years. Water that is stored improperly can become contaminated with bacteria, algae, or chemicals from the storage container itself. That's why it's critical to follow these best practices for maintaining water quality:

1. Use Food-Grade Containers: Always store water in containers that are specifically designed for water storage. Avoid using containers that previously held chemicals or non-food substances, as they could leach toxins into the water over time.

2. Disinfect Water Before Storing: If you're filling your own containers, make sure to disinfect the water by adding 8 drops of unscented household bleach (per gallon) to kill any bacteria. Alternatively, you can purchase water purification tablets for long-term storage.

3. Store in a Cool, Dark Place: Water should be stored away from direct sunlight and in a cool area to prevent algae growth and slow the degradation of plastic containers. Basements, garages, or utility rooms are ideal locations for water storage.

4. Rotate Water Supplies: Even properly stored water should be rotated every 6 to 12 months to ensure freshness. Use your oldest water first and replenish with fresh water to maintain an ongoing supply.

Building Redundancy: Combining Storage with Renewable Water Sources

While storing water is essential, relying solely on stored water during a long-term crisis can be challenging. For Jack, who prioritizes resilience, combining water storage with renewable sources like rainwater harvesting or access to a well or natural spring is the best way to ensure long-term survival.

In addition to having large water storage containers, setting up a rainwater harvesting system allows you to continually replenish your water supply. This not only extends the lifespan of your stored water but also reduces the pressure to rely on limited resources. As mentioned in previous sections, filtering and purifying this water is essential to ensure it's safe for consumption.

Jack might also explore local water sources such as nearby lakes or rivers, especially if he has access to portable water filtration devices or UV purifiers to treat the water. Having redundancy built into his water plan will make him far less vulnerable to running out of water in a long-term emergency.

Contingency Planning for Water Loss

Even with a well-prepared water storage plan, unforeseen circumstances can lead to water loss. Whether it's contamination, leaks, or theft, having a backup plan for securing additional water is key. Consider the following contingency strategies:

- **Portable Water Filters:** In the event of a storage failure, having portable water filters on hand can allow you to safely collect and purify water from local sources.
- **Rainwater Collection:** Set up multiple rain barrels around your property to collect and store rainwater for emergencies. This gives you a renewable source of water.
- **Water Purification Tablets:** Keep a supply of chemical water purification tablets in your emergency kit to treat any suspect water.

Identifying Local Water Sources

In a crisis or off-grid scenario, your stored water may not always be sufficient to meet your household's needs. For Jack, who prioritizes preparedness and long-term self-sufficiency, identifying local water sources becomes essential. Understanding where to find reliable water sources near your home, and how to safely access them, can make a significant difference in your ability to survive extended emergencies. This chapter will explore different local water sources, how to identify them, and what precautions to take when utilizing them for drinking, hygiene, or cooking.

Types of Local Water Sources

When it comes to finding water locally, several natural and man-made sources may be available, depending on your environment. It's important to familiarize yourself with these options before a crisis hits, as the ability to collect and purify water from local sources could be the key to your survival.

Natural Water Sources

Rivers and Streams: Flowing water sources like rivers and streams are often the most accessible option for people living in proximity to rural or wooded areas. Flowing water generally has fewer contaminants than stagnant sources, but it still requires thorough purification to remove bacteria, parasites, and potential chemical pollutants. Streams that originate from springs or higher altitudes are often cleaner than those that flow through heavily populated or agricultural areas.

Lakes and Ponds: Still water bodies like lakes and ponds are also viable water sources, though they typically contain more sediment, algae, and other biological contaminants. When using water from these sources, it's important to let it settle and use filtration to remove particulates before moving on to purification.

Rainwater: Though rainwater can be harvested directly through a rainwater harvesting system, you may also be able to collect rainwater in an emergency by using tarps, buckets, or any other materials to funnel the water into a storage container. While rainwater is often cleaner than surface water from lakes or rivers, it still requires purification to remove airborne contaminants or pollutants that may have been picked up during the collection process.

Springs: One of the best natural water sources, springs bring groundwater to the surface, often providing clean and drinkable water. In many rural or mountainous areas, natural springs are highly prized for their purity. However, even spring water should be purified if you're unsure of its cleanliness or if it's exposed to surface contaminants.

Snow and Ice: In cold climates, snow and ice can be excellent water sources, but there are important considerations to keep in mind. Melted snow provides safe drinking water if purified, but never eat snow directly as it can lower your core body temperature and lead to hypothermia. Be sure to melt and purify snow or ice before drinking it.

Man-Made Water Sources

In urban or suburban settings, natural water sources may be limited or difficult to access. However, man-made options can be lifesaving during a crisis.

Wells: If you have a private well, you already have access to one of the best water sources available during an emergency. Wells tap into groundwater, which is typically cleaner than surface water, but it's still important to test and purify well water before drinking it if contamination is suspected. Some communities may also have public wells, especially in rural areas, which can be used as an emergency water source.

Cisterns: Some homes, particularly in areas prone to drought, are equipped with cisterns that store rainwater or well water. If your home has a cistern, this can provide an additional layer of water security during a crisis. However, cistern water must be monitored for contamination and purified before use.

Swimming Pools: In a true emergency, swimming pool water can be a valuable resource for non-potable uses such as bathing, washing, or flushing toilets. While chlorine in pool water kills many harmful organisms, it isn't suitable for drinking unless it's thoroughly purified and treated, as chlorine can cause adverse health effects in high concentrations.

Water Heaters and Plumbing Systems: Water stored in your home's water heater or pipes can be another emergency resource. In the event of a water outage, drain the tank for immediate access. While this water is generally safe to drink if your plumbing system is clean, it's wise to purify it before consumption.

How to Find Local Water Sources

Identifying local water sources in advance will save valuable time during a crisis. Here's how you can assess and prepare to use local water sources effectively:

1. Research Local Geography: Use topographical maps or geographic information system (GIS) tools to locate nearby rivers, lakes, and springs. These tools can help you pinpoint water sources that may not be immediately visible, like hidden springs or remote streams.

2. Speak with Locals: In rural areas, long-time residents may know about hidden springs or lesser-known water sources. It's valuable to establish connections with your neighbors and community to share knowledge about local resources.

3. Observe Terrain: Understanding the lay of the land can also help you find water sources. For example, water tends to collect in low-lying areas or depressions in the terrain. Look for green vegetation in otherwise dry landscapes, as this often signals the presence of underground water.

4. Search for Wildlife Activity: Animals need water too, and their presence can indicate nearby sources. Trails worn by animals often lead to water, so be observant of wildlife behavior in your area.

Safety Precautions When Collecting Water

While finding a local water source is essential, it's equally important to know how to safely collect and purify the water before using it for drinking or hygiene. Untreated water can contain harmful microorganisms like giardia, E. coli, or chemical pollutants that could put your family's health at risk.

1. Always Filter and Purify: Never assume that a water source is safe to drink without filtration and purification. Even crystal-clear water from mountain streams or springs can harbor harmful bacteria or viruses. A portable water filter combined with a UV purifier or chemical treatment (like iodine or chlorine tablets) is essential when dealing with unknown water sources.

2. Avoid Stagnant Water: Standing or slow-moving water, like in ponds or shallow pools, tends to accumulate more contaminants than fast-moving water. It's always better to collect water from flowing sources such as rivers, streams, or springs when possible.

3. Test Well Water: If you're relying on a well, test the water periodically for bacterial contamination or chemical pollutants. In an emergency, where professional testing isn't possible, use purification techniques such as boiling or chlorination to ensure the water is safe for consumption.

4. Prevent Cross-Contamination: When collecting water from an outdoor source, use dedicated containers and avoid allowing the container's mouth to touch the water directly. This helps prevent cross-contamination and keeps your collected water as clean as possible before purification.

Tools and Gear for Collecting Water

Having the right tools and gear in your emergency kit is critical to efficiently collect water from local sources. Some key items include:

*   **Portable Water Filters:** Lightweight filters that remove bacteria and protozoa from water are ideal for collecting water on the go.
*   **Collapsible Water Containers:** These are great for carrying larger quantities of water from a source back to your home.
*   **UV Water Purifiers:** These devices are fast and effective at killing pathogens, making them a valuable tool for ensuring water safety.
*   **Buckets or Tarps:** Simple items like buckets and tarps can be used to collect rainwater during a storm or to gather water from shallow sources.

CHAPTER 4

LONG-TERM FOOD STORAGE AND PREPARATION

- -

Stockpiling the Right Foods for Extended Crises

When planning for a long-term crisis, stockpiling food is a cornerstone of survival. The ability to maintain a steady supply of nutritious, calorie-dense foods that can last for months—or even years—without spoiling is critical for ensuring the well-being of your family. For Jack, the goal of building a robust food stockpile means choosing foods that are not only long-lasting but also nutritionally balanced and versatile enough to meet the needs of his household over an extended period.

This section will dive deep into how to stockpile the right foods, what types of food to focus on, and how to ensure that your stockpile is sustainable and manageable, even during an extended crisis.

The Principles of Long-Term Food Storage

Before diving into specific foods, it's essential to understand the basic principles behind long-term food storage. The goal is to select foods that are:

- **Non-perishable:** These are foods that can last for months or years without spoiling. The longevity of these items makes them essential in a survival pantry.

- **Nutritionally balanced:** Stockpiling food that is both calorie-dense and rich in essential nutrients ensures that your family stays healthy even when access to fresh food is limited.

- **Easy to store:** Foods that are compact, lightweight, and easy to store in various conditions are ideal for long-term stockpiling.

- **Versatile:** Foods that can be used in a variety of meals provide flexibility, making it easier to avoid meal fatigue during long-term survival scenarios.

With these principles in mind, let's explore the key types of food to prioritize when building a survival pantry.

Non-Perishable Staples

The foundation of any long-term food stockpile is non-perishable staples. These foods are known for their incredibly long shelf lives and can form the bulk of your diet during an extended crisis. They are typically calorie-dense, providing the energy needed to sustain physical activity, maintain mental focus, and ensure overall well-being.

GRAINS AND LEGUMES

Grains and legumes are some of the most important foods to stockpile because they are versatile, inexpensive, and can be stored for many years. Whole grains such as rice, oats, wheat berries, and quinoa provide a significant source of carbohydrates, the body's primary energy source. These grains can be stored in airtight containers with oxygen absorbers to extend their shelf life for up to 25 years when stored properly.

Legumes, including dried beans, lentils, and split peas, are another essential component of a long-term stockpile. They are rich in protein and fiber, making them a key source of nutrition in the absence of fresh meat or dairy. Additionally, legumes are easy to cook and can be incorporated into a wide variety of meals, from soups and stews to simple side dishes.

RICE

Among grains, white rice stands out as one of the best options for long-term storage. When stored in Mylar bags with oxygen absorbers, white rice can last up to 30 years. It's a staple in many cultures and can be easily combined with other stockpiled foods to create a satisfying, energy-boosting meal.

CANNED GOODS

Canned foods offer convenience and a long shelf life, making them an essential part of your stockpile. Look for a variety of canned goods, including:

- **Vegetables:** Canned vegetables like green beans, corn, carrots, and peas provide essential vitamins and minerals when fresh produce is unavailable.
- **Fruits:** Canned fruits, especially those packed in water or natural juices, offer a reliable source of vitamin C and fiber.
- **Proteins:** Canned meats such as tuna, chicken, salmon, and even spam are excellent protein sources that can last several years in storage. Other protein options include canned beans and nut butters like peanut butter, which offer plant-based protein.

Canned goods should be stored in a cool, dry place, and it's important to rotate your stock regularly to ensure freshness. While they are not as lightweight as dehydrated foods, their convenience and ease of preparation make them invaluable during an emergency.

Dehydrated and Freeze-Dried Foods

Another excellent option for long-term food storage is dehydrated or freeze-dried foods. These foods have had their moisture removed, which dramatically increases their shelf life and reduces their weight, making them easy to store and transport.

- **Dehydrated fruits and vegetables:** Dehydrated produce retains most of its nutrients and can be rehydrated with water to make soups, stews, or side dishes. Items like dehydrated potatoes, apples, carrots, and peppers are particularly useful in survival situations, providing essential vitamins and minerals.
- **Freeze-dried meals:** Freeze-dried meals, available in many emergency food kits, are convenient because they only require the addition of hot water to prepare. Brands like Mountain House or Wise Company offer a variety of meals, from breakfast options like oatmeal to more substantial dishes like pasta, chili, or beef stew.

Freeze-dried foods typically last between 20 to 30 years when stored correctly, and they are often available in bulk quantities, making them a great option for those looking to build a large, sustainable stockpile.

Proteins and Fats

While carbohydrates are essential for energy, your body also needs protein and fats for muscle maintenance, brain function, and hormone production. In an extended crisis, access to fresh meat, eggs, or dairy may be limited, so it's important to have a plan in place to provide these nutrients.

- **Canned or freeze-dried meat:** As mentioned, canned meats like tuna, chicken, and salmon are excellent protein sources. Freeze-dried meat, such as beef or chicken, offers the same benefits with a much longer shelf life.
- **Powdered eggs and dairy:** Powdered eggs and powdered milk are invaluable in an emergency pantry. These can be used in baking or for cooking, and they provide a much-needed source of protein and calcium.
- **Nuts and seeds:** Almonds, peanuts, sunflower seeds, and flaxseeds are rich in healthy fats, protein, and fiber. Vacuum-sealed or stored with oxygen absorbers, these can last for several years without spoiling.
- **Cooking oils:** While oils do have a shorter shelf life compared to other foods, it's important to include olive oil, coconut oil, or ghee in your stockpile. These provide the fats necessary for cooking and baking, as well as an essential source of calories. To extend their longevity, store them in a cool, dark place, and aim to use them within a year or two of purchase.

Supplements and Vitamins

During extended crises, your diet may not be as varied or balanced as it would be under normal circumstances. To ensure your family remains healthy, consider adding vitamin supplements to your stockpile. Multivitamins can help fill the gaps in your diet, particularly when fresh fruits and vegetables are scarce.

Additionally, look into electrolyte powders or sports drinks that can help prevent dehydration and replace essential minerals lost through sweat.

DIY Food Preservation Methods

In a long-term crisis, the ability to preserve your own food can be the difference between survival and scarcity. Stockpiling non-perishable foods is only part of the equation; knowing how to effectively preserve fresh produce, meat, and dairy is an invaluable skill that gives you control over your food supply, even when external resources are unavailable. Jack, whose top priority is ensuring his family's readiness, recognizes the value of mastering DIY food preservation techniques. These methods not only extend the shelf life of food but also maintain its nutritional value, allowing his family to stay healthy in any situation.

In this section, we'll explore several practical food preservation methods, each of which is feasible with basic equipment and minimal resources. From dehydration to fermentation, these techniques will enable Jack to make the most out of every food item he stores or grows.

Dehydration

One of the simplest and most effective ways to preserve food is through dehydration. This method removes the moisture from food, preventing the growth of bacteria, mold, and yeast, which are responsible for spoilage. By drying foods like fruits, vegetables, and meats, you can extend their shelf life significantly while retaining much of their nutritional content.

HOW TO DEHYDRATE FOODS

Dehydration can be done using several methods, including air drying, oven drying, or using a food dehydrator. While each method works, a dedicated food dehydrator is often the most efficient and reliable option for long-term food preservation.

- **Fruits:** Common fruits like apples, bananas, berries, and mangoes can be sliced and dehydrated into lightweight, easy-to-store snacks. Dried fruits maintain their natural sugars, making them a great energy-boosting food during emergencies.
- **Vegetables:** Vegetables like carrots, zucchini, tomatoes, and mushrooms can also be dried and stored. Once rehydrated, they can be used in soups, stews, or casseroles.
- **Meats:** Dehydrated meats, commonly referred to as jerky, are a great source of protein in survival situations. Lean cuts of beef, turkey, or venison are ideal for making jerky, as the low-fat content ensures a longer shelf life.

Once dehydrated, foods should be stored in airtight containers with oxygen absorbers or vacuum-sealed bags to keep them fresh for months or even years.

Canning

Canning is another popular method for preserving food, particularly when you have an abundance of fresh fruits or vegetables. This process involves sealing food in glass jars and heating them to a high temperature, which kills bacteria and creates a vacuum seal that prevents further contamination. Canned goods can last for several years if stored in a cool, dark place, making this an ideal method for long-term survival preparation.

Water Bath Canning vs. Pressure Canning

There are two primary methods of canning: water bath canning and pressure canning.

- **Water bath canning:** This method is used for high-acid foods such as fruits, pickles, jams, and tomatoes. The natural acidity in these foods helps prevent the growth of harmful bacteria. Water bath canning is a relatively simple process and requires only a large pot of boiling water and some canning jars.
- **Pressure canning:** For low-acid foods like vegetables, meats, and legumes, pressure canning is necessary. These foods require higher temperatures to kill bacteria, including botulism, which thrives in low-acid environments. A pressure canner allows you to reach these temperatures, ensuring that your food is safely preserved for long-term storage.

Canning is a more involved process compared to dehydration, but it's an excellent way to preserve hearty meals like stews, soups, or chili, which can be ready to eat with minimal preparation during an emergency.

Fermentation

Fermentation is one of the oldest and most natural ways to preserve food. This process relies on beneficial bacteria to convert sugars into lactic acid, which acts as a natural preservative. Fermented foods are not only long-lasting, but they are also rich in probiotics, which promote gut health and help boost the immune system—critical benefits during a crisis when maintaining health is paramount.

Foods to Ferment

- **Vegetables:** Common vegetables for fermentation include cabbage, cucumbers, carrots, and radishes. Sauerkraut and kimchi are well-known examples of fermented cabbage, but many other vegetables can be fermented to create nutrient-dense, probiotic-rich foods.
- **Dairy:** Milk can be fermented into products like yogurt, kefir, and cheese. These foods

provide a great source of protein and calcium, both of which are important in a crisis scenario where fresh dairy may be scarce.

- **Grains:** Certain grains, like sourdough, can also be fermented. Fermentation makes grains easier to digest and improves their nutritional profile, which can be beneficial when your diet is limited to stored foods.

Fermentation is relatively easy to do at home with basic supplies. Vegetables are typically fermented in salt brine, while dairy products require specific cultures to initiate the fermentation process. Fermented foods should be stored in a cool place to slow down the fermentation process and prolong their shelf life.

Freezing

While freezing may not be the first method that comes to mind for long-term survival, it can be an effective short to medium-term preservation technique if you have access to a reliable power source or backup generator. Freezing locks in nutrients and freshness, making it a great option for preserving a wide variety of foods, from meats to fruits and vegetables.

How to Freeze Food Properly

To maximize the longevity of frozen foods, follow these steps:

- **Blanch vegetables:** Blanching (quickly boiling and then cooling vegetables) helps retain their color, flavor, and nutritional value before freezing.
- **Use freezer-safe packaging:** Always use freezer bags, vacuum-sealed bags, or freezer-safe containers to prevent freezer burn. Remove as much air as possible from the packaging to ensure that the food stays fresh.
- **Label everything:** Be sure to label all frozen items with the date of freezing and what's inside. Rotating your frozen food supply and using the oldest items first ensures nothing is wasted.

While freezing is convenient, it's important to have a backup plan in place, such as a generator, to keep your freezer running in case of a power outage. Jack knows the importance of redundancy, so having frozen foods in combination with other preservation methods ensures his family always has something to fall back on.

Pickling

Pickling is a form of food preservation that uses vinegar or brine to preserve fruits and vegetables. The high acidity in vinegar prevents bacteria growth, making it a reliable and easy method to preserve produce for several months. Pickled foods retain their flavor and crunch, offering variety to your diet during long-term crises when fresh vegetables may be hard to come by.

FOODS TO PICKLE

Vegetables like cucumbers, carrots, peppers, and beets are commonly pickled, but fruits like pears or peaches can also be preserved this way. Pickled foods offer a tangy, refreshing contrast to the often bland nature of survival foods, making them a welcome addition to any stockpile.

Pickling is also an easy DIY method that requires minimal equipment. With just vinegar, salt, and some basic spices, you can create pickled foods that last for months in your pantry. As long as the jars are properly sealed, pickled foods will remain shelf-stable and ready to eat when needed.

Rotating and Monitoring Your Food Supply

When stockpiling food for long-term crises, it's not enough to simply amass supplies and forget about them. The key to maintaining a viable and sustainable stockpile is regular rotation and careful monitoring. By ensuring that your food stores are consistently rotated and checked for spoilage, you can avoid waste, maintain food safety, and ensure that your family is always consuming the freshest supplies available.

Jack, who prioritizes a systematic approach to preparedness, understands the importance of keeping his food stockpile organized and properly monitored. In this section, we'll explore strategies for rotating and monitoring your food supply to ensure it remains effective during any long-term crisis.

Why Food Rotation Is Critical

Food rotation is essential for several reasons, all of which contribute to the longevity, quality, and safety of your stockpile:

- **Preventing spoilage:** Even non-perishable foods have a shelf life, and if left unchecked, they can spoil or lose their nutritional value over time. Rotation ensures that older items are used first, reducing the likelihood of waste.

- **Maximizing nutritional value:** Foods that are closer to their expiration date may still be safe to eat, but they may have lost some of their original nutritional value. By consuming your stockpile in a timely manner, you ensure your family is getting the maximum benefit from each food item.

- **Maintaining variety:** Rotating your food supply also allows you to introduce fresh stock regularly, helping to maintain variety in your meals. This reduces the risk of "food fatigue," where the monotony of eating the same foods over an extended period leads to a decline in morale and appetite.

The First In, First Out (FIFO) System

One of the simplest and most effective ways to manage your food rotation is by implementing the First In, First Out (FIFO) system. This method ensures that older stock is used before newer items, reducing the risk of food spoilage and waste. Here's how to set up a FIFO system in your home:

1. Label everything: Begin by labeling each item in your stockpile with the date it was purchased or stored. This can be done with permanent markers or color-coded labels that allow you to easily track the age of your supplies.

2. Organize by expiration date: Arrange your food storage area so that items closest to their expiration date are at the front, while newer items are stored at the back. This way, when you're ready to use an item, you'll naturally grab the older stock first.

3. Rotate new stock in: Whenever you add new supplies to your stockpile, take the time to move older items forward and place the fresh stock at the back. This process may seem tedious, but it ensures that nothing goes to waste and that you're always consuming the freshest available food.

4. Check dates regularly: It's important to regularly check the expiration dates of your stockpile and to be aware of the shelf life of each item. Some foods, like canned goods, may last years, while others, like dried fruits or oils, may have a shorter shelf life and should be monitored more closely.

Monitoring Your Stockpile for Spoilage

In addition to rotating your food, it's essential to consistently monitor your stockpile for signs of spoilage. Even foods with long shelf lives can become contaminated or go bad if not stored properly. To ensure that your food remains safe to consume, follow these best practices for monitoring:

- **Inspect cans and jars:** Check canned goods for any signs of bulging, dents, or rust, as these can be indicators of bacterial growth or compromised seals. Bulging cans are a clear sign of spoilage, and any can exhibiting these symptoms should be discarded immediately.

- **Look for mold or discoloration:** Dried foods, such as grains or legumes, should be checked for any visible signs of mold or discoloration. If you notice any off-color spots or unusual textures, it's better to discard the item than risk contamination.

- **Check for pests:** Pests like weevils, moths, or rodents can infiltrate food storage areas, especially if items are not stored in sealed, airtight containers. Regularly inspect your stockpile for signs of infestation, such as small holes in packaging, droppings, or live insects. Using oxygen absorbers or storing food in vacuum-sealed bags can help prevent infestations.

- **Smell and taste:** When in doubt, use your senses. If a food item smells off or tastes strange, it's safer to discard it than take the risk of consuming spoiled food.

Record-Keeping and Inventory Management

Jack knows that a well-maintained inventory system is crucial for keeping track of his family's food supply. Keeping detailed records of what's in your stockpile, when it was added, and its expiration date allows you to stay on top of rotation and ensure that no food goes to waste.

There are a few ways to manage your food inventory effectively:

- **Manual logs:** Keeping a simple written log of your inventory is an easy, low-tech solution that requires minimal resources. Record each item's name, quantity, date of purchase, and expiration date. Be sure to update the log whenever you add new stock or use items from the pantry.
- **Digital inventory apps:** For those who prefer a more tech-savvy solution, inventory management apps designed specifically for preppers or homemakers can streamline the process. These apps allow you to create digital logs of your food supplies, set reminders for when items are nearing their expiration date, and even categorize foods based on type and shelf life. Some apps even include barcode scanning, making it easy to input new items with just a scan of the label.
- **Visual methods:** If you prefer a more visual approach, use color-coded labels or sticky notes to help identify which foods are nearing their expiration date. This method is especially useful if you have a large stockpile spread across multiple locations, such as a basement pantry and a garage storage area.

Best Practices for Long-Term Food Rotation

To keep your stockpile running smoothly, here are a few best practices that will help you stay organized and ensure your food remains fresh:

- **Use it regularly:** Don't let your food stockpile sit untouched for months on end. Incorporate items from your stockpile into your regular meals to keep your rotation system active. This also allows you to familiarize yourself with the foods you've stored and ensures you know how to prepare them in an emergency.
- **Store food in multiple locations:** Spread your stockpile across different areas of your home. This not only protects your food from localized damage (such as a flood in the basement) but also makes it easier to rotate and access different parts of your supply.
- **Plan meals around your stockpile:** Regularly plan meals that incorporate foods close to their expiration date. This helps prevent waste while keeping your stockpile refreshed. Simple meals like soups, stews, or casseroles are great ways to use a variety of items from your pantry.

Preparing for Emergency Scenarios

Rotating and monitoring your food supply becomes even more important in a long-term crisis when restocking may not be an option. Jack, for example, plans to regularly review his stockpile and keep an up-to-date list of what's available, ensuring that his family is always prepared. By staying on top of food rotation, Jack can prevent spoilage, maintain a nutritionally balanced supply, and be confident that his family will have access to safe, reliable food during extended emergencies.

Gardening and Growing Your Own Food

In times of long-term crises or extended survival situations, the ability to grow your own food becomes more than a simple convenience—it's a vital skill for maintaining self-sufficiency and ensuring your family's long-term survival. Jack, who is meticulous in his approach to preparedness, understands that having a sustainable food source goes beyond stockpiling non-perishables. Gardening, when done effectively, can provide an ongoing supply of fresh produce that replenishes your food stores while promoting health and independence.

This section delves into the practicalities of gardening and growing your own food, covering everything from selecting the right crops to setting up your garden and maintaining it over time. It's a skill that requires patience, knowledge, and careful planning, but the rewards are well worth the effort when fresh food becomes scarce.

Choosing the Right Crops for Survival Gardening

The first step in starting your survival garden is selecting the right crops. Not all plants are suitable for long-term survival scenarios, so it's important to choose crops that are nutrient-dense, easy to grow, and hardy enough to withstand various environmental conditions. Additionally, you'll want crops that can produce high yields and store well.

Some of the best crops for a survival garden include:

- **Potatoes:** These are a survival garden staple. They are rich in carbohydrates, easy to grow, and store well. Potatoes can be grown in the ground or even in containers, making them versatile for different gardening spaces.
- **Beans:** Beans are another essential crop because they provide a great source of protein and fiber. They can be grown as bush beans or pole beans, depending on the space you have. Dried beans store well and can last for years.
- **Tomatoes:** Not only are tomatoes easy to grow, but they also provide a wealth of vitamins and can be used in various recipes. Tomatoes are also ideal for canning, which further extends their shelf life.
- **Carrots and Beets:** Root vegetables like carrots and beets are excellent for long-term food security. They are nutrient-dense and store well when properly harvested and stored in cool conditions.
- **Leafy Greens:** Kale, spinach, and Swiss chard are nutrient powerhouses that grow quickly and can be harvested multiple times throughout their growing season.

- **Herbs:** Herbs like basil, rosemary, thyme, and oregano not only enhance the flavor of your meals but also provide medicinal benefits. Herbs are easy to grow and can be dried for long-term storage.

When planning your garden, think about crops that are calorie-dense and high in essential nutrients like vitamins, proteins, and minerals. Diversity is key, as it ensures a wide range of nutrients while preventing boredom with your meals.

Setting Up Your Survival Garden

Once you've selected the right crops, the next step is to plan and set up your garden. The size of your garden will depend on the available space and the number of people you're feeding, but it's important to think about sustainability and efficiency.

RAISED BEDS VS. TRADITIONAL ROWS

Many survival gardeners choose to grow their crops in raised beds, which offer several advantages over traditional row planting. Raised beds provide better drainage, prevent soil compaction, and make it easier to control the quality of the soil. They are also easier to protect from pests and can be covered with row covers or greenhouses to extend the growing season.

However, if you have the space and the right soil, traditional row planting is another option, particularly for crops like corn, potatoes, or squash that take up more room. Whichever method you choose, be sure to plan your garden layout to maximize space and efficiency.

COMPANION PLANTING

Another useful technique to consider is companion planting, which involves planting crops that benefit each other when grown together. For example:

- Tomatoes grow well alongside basil, which helps repel pests that typically target tomatoes.
- Beans can be grown with corn, as the beans fix nitrogen in the soil, which benefits the corn, and the corn provides support for the bean vines.
- Marigolds are great companions for most vegetables as they deter many harmful insects and pests from the garden.

Using these types of symbiotic planting techniques can increase the yield of your garden while reducing the need for chemical fertilizers or pesticides.

Watering and Soil Management

Your survival garden's success depends heavily on maintaining proper soil health and providing consistent water. Start by testing your soil to ensure it has the right pH and nutrient levels. Adding compost or manure can improve soil fertility, helping your plants grow stronger and yield more.

Watering is equally important, and in a survival situation, conserving water is key. Jack would benefit from installing a rainwater harvesting system to provide a consistent water supply for his garden, especially during droughts or water shortages. Drip irrigation systems, which deliver water directly to the roots of your plants, are highly efficient and reduce water waste.

Mulching is another effective way to maintain soil moisture and prevent weeds. By covering the soil with organic material like straw or wood chips, you can help the soil retain moisture longer, reducing the need for frequent watering.

Extending the Growing Season

In many climates, the growing season is limited, but there are several strategies Jack can employ to extend the harvest period and increase his garden's productivity:

- **Greenhouses:** A greenhouse allows you to grow crops year-round, regardless of outside temperatures. Even a small, DIY greenhouse can make a huge difference in keeping tender plants alive through the winter months.
- **Cold Frames:** Cold frames are another great option for extending the growing season. These simple structures protect plants from frost and allow you to start seeds earlier in the spring or continue growing vegetables late into the fall.
- **Row Covers:** Lightweight row covers can be draped over plants to protect them from frost and pests. They are inexpensive and easy to use, making them a practical addition to any survival garden.

Harvesting and Storing Your Produce

Knowing when and how to harvest your crops is critical to ensuring a steady supply of food throughout the year. Different crops have different harvesting timelines, so it's important to familiarize yourself with the specific needs of each plant in your garden.

Once harvested, crops should be preserved as soon as possible. Root vegetables like potatoes, carrots, and beets can be stored in a cool, dark location, such as a root cellar, where they can last for several months. Leafy greens and herbs can be dried or frozen, while tomatoes and beans can be canned or freeze-dried.

For Jack, growing and preserving his own food will ensure a continuous and reliable food supply that supplements his stockpiled goods. It also provides a sense of self-reliance and independence, which are core to his preparedness philosophy.

The Mental and Physical Benefits of Gardening

Beyond the practical benefits of providing food, gardening has numerous mental and physical health benefits. For Jack and his family, growing their own food can serve as a way to reduce stress, stay active, and feel empowered during difficult times. Gardening is an excellent form of low-impact exercise that keeps the body moving and improves overall fitness, while the act of caring for plants and watching them grow fosters a sense of purpose and achievement.

In a long-term crisis, maintaining positive mental health is just as important as physical survival, and gardening offers a productive, grounding activity that supports both. By growing his own food, Jack ensures that his family's needs are met while creating a routine that fosters resilience and well-being in the face of uncertainty.

Hunting, Fishing, and Foraging

In a long-term survival scenario, relying solely on stored food supplies may not be sufficient to sustain you and your family indefinitely. Jack understands that the key to self-reliance is supplementing his food stores with natural resources available in the environment. Hunting, fishing, and foraging are ancient, time-tested methods of gathering food that have allowed humans to thrive in a variety of ecosystems. These skills not only provide a renewable food source but also offer an essential connection to the natural world, fostering self-sufficiency and resilience in times of crisis.

This section explores the practical aspects of hunting, fishing, and foraging, focusing on how Jack can leverage these skills to ensure his family's long-term food security during an extended emergency.

Hunting for Sustainable Protein

Hunting is one of the most efficient ways to secure high-quality, sustainable protein in a survival situation. Wild game provides a rich source of calories, fats, and nutrients that are essential for maintaining strength and health, particularly during physically demanding periods. Learning how to effectively hunt and process wild animals ensures that Jack can provide fresh meat for his family without depending on dwindling stockpiles of canned or freeze-dried protein.

What to Hunt

The animals available to hunt will depend largely on Jack's geographical location, but there are several common species that are ideal for survival hunting due to their abundance and nutritional value:

- **Deer:** In many regions, white-tailed deer or mule deer are plentiful and provide a large amount of meat from a single kill. A single deer can provide up to 50-75 pounds of meat, which can be preserved for long-term storage through smoking, drying, or freezing.

- **Rabbits and squirrels:** Small game like rabbits and squirrels are abundant in both rural and suburban areas, making them accessible for most hunters. They are easy to trap or hunt with minimal equipment and can be a steady source of protein throughout the year.

- **Wild boar:** In areas where wild boar populations have grown, these animals can be hunted as a source of large quantities of meat. Wild boar are aggressive and require careful handling, but they offer a nutrient-rich food source that can be smoked, dried, or frozen for future use.

- **Waterfowl and birds:** Ducks, geese, and other waterfowl provide both meat and fat, which are valuable in survival situations. Smaller birds like pheasants, quail, and doves are also relatively easy to hunt or trap and can provide a steady supply of protein.

Hunting requires the proper equipment, including firearms, bows, or traps, as well as knowledge of the local wildlife and hunting regulations. Jack will need to familiarize himself with the species in his area and learn the best times of year for hunting, as well as how to field dress and process his game to ensure the meat is safe to eat.

Fishing for a Renewable Food Source

Fishing offers another renewable source of protein, particularly for those living near rivers, lakes, or coastal areas. Fish are rich in omega-3 fatty acids, protein, and essential nutrients, making them an important addition to any survival diet. Fishing also requires less energy than hunting and can provide a continuous food supply throughout the year, depending on the body of water.

FISHING TECHNIQUES

For Jack, having multiple fishing techniques in his arsenal will increase his chances of success, regardless of the type of water he's fishing in:

- **Rod and reel fishing:** This traditional method is simple and effective for catching fish in most environments. Using a basic fishing rod with a variety of baits and lures will allow Jack to catch a range of fish, from small panfish to larger species like bass or catfish.

- **Trotlines and fish traps:** For more passive fishing, trotlines and fish traps can be set up in rivers or lakes to catch fish while Jack focuses on other survival tasks. These methods are particularly useful in times of crisis, as they allow for fishing without constant attention.

- **Spearfishing:** In shallow waters or coastal areas, spearfishing with a homemade spear or gig can be an effective way to catch fish, especially if Jack has some experience with this technique. Spearfishing requires patience and skill, but it can yield valuable protein in environments where other methods may not work.

Fishing gear, such as fishing line, hooks, nets, and weights, should be included in Jack's survival kit. Additionally, learning how to make improvised fishing gear from available materials will further enhance his ability to gather food in the wild.

Foraging for Edible Plants

While hunting and fishing are essential for protein, foraging offers a way to gather additional nutrients from wild plants. Foraging requires knowledge of local plant species, as some are highly nutritious while others may be toxic. In a long-term crisis, Jack can supplement his diet with wild fruits, vegetables, nuts, and medicinal herbs found in the surrounding environment.

EDIBLE PLANTS TO FORAGE

Depending on the region, there are several common plants that are safe to forage and provide essential vitamins and minerals:

- **Wild berries:** Blackberries, raspberries, blueberries, and strawberries grow in many regions and are rich in antioxidants, vitamins, and fiber. These berries can be eaten fresh or preserved by drying or canning for future use.
- **Nuts and seeds:** Acorns, walnuts, hazelnuts, and pecans are valuable sources of protein and healthy fats. These can be gathered in the fall and stored for long-term consumption. Acorns, in particular, can be processed into flour after leaching out the tannins.
- **Dandelion and plantain:** Common yard plants like dandelion and plantain are highly nutritious and versatile. Dandelion leaves can be eaten in salads or cooked, while the roots can be used to make tea. Plantain is a wild herb that can be used in soups or as a medicinal herb to treat wounds and inflammation.
- **Mushrooms:** Wild mushrooms can be a valuable food source, but Jack must be cautious when foraging them. Some mushrooms are highly toxic, so it's essential to have a thorough knowledge of safe species. Morels, chanterelles, and puffballs are commonly foraged mushrooms that provide vitamins and minerals.
- **Herbs and greens:** Wild herbs like mint, oregano, and chickweed can be found in many environments. These plants not only enhance the flavor of meals but also provide medicinal benefits. Chickweed and purslane, for instance, are edible weeds that are packed with nutrients and can be eaten raw or cooked.

Foraging offers a sustainable way to diversify the diet and introduce fresh, nutrient-rich foods into the survival plan. However, Jack must be cautious about identifying plants correctly, as misidentification can lead to illness or worse. A field guide to local edible plants is an essential tool in any survival kit.

Preserving the Food You Hunt, Fish, and Forage

Once Jack has successfully gathered food through hunting, fishing, or foraging, the next challenge is preserving it for long-term storage. Smoking, drying, and canning are the primary methods for preserving meat, fish, and foraged plants.

- **Smoking meat and fish:** Smoking adds flavor and extends the shelf life of game meat and fish by removing moisture and preventing bacterial growth. This method can be done with a simple DIY smoker, and the preserved food can last for several months.

- **Drying herbs and fruits:** Drying is an easy way to preserve foraged herbs, berries, and edible greens. Dried foods take up little space and can be stored for long periods in airtight containers.

- **Canning:** Foragers and hunters alike benefit from canning their harvests. Wild fruits, vegetables, and even meats can be preserved through canning, providing a ready-to-eat food supply during the winter or lean times.

CHAPTER 5
MENTAL PREPARATION AND RESILIENCE

- -

Developing a Navy SEAL Mindset

One of the most critical aspects of survival is not just the physical preparedness, but the mental resilience required to face high-stress scenarios. The Navy SEAL mindset is built on years of intense training, perseverance, and a commitment to never giving up, no matter how dire the circumstances. This mental fortitude is something that anyone can develop, with the right focus and training. Jack, a family man preparing for potential crises, understands that cultivating this mindset will help not only him but his family stay grounded and determined when facing long-term challenges.

The Navy SEAL mindset is not just about physical strength or tactical skills; it's about mastering one's mind, emotions, and reactions to adversity. To survive in extreme conditions, Jack must learn to tap into this same unshakeable mental strength.

The Core Principles of the Navy SEAL Mindset

The foundation of the Navy SEAL mentality is based on several key principles that can be applied to anyone's life, even outside the battlefield. These principles enable individuals to face fear, manage stress, and continue performing under immense pressure. Jack can benefit from incorporating these tenets into his survival preparations, ensuring he stays focused and resilient during a crisis.

MENTAL TOUGHNESS

Mental toughness is at the heart of the Navy SEAL ethos. SEALs are trained to push beyond their physical and mental limits, enduring conditions that would break most people. This same toughness can be developed through exposure to uncomfortable situations and learning how to stay calm under pressure. For Jack, this means pushing himself and his family beyond their comfort zones. Whether it's physical challenges like endurance training or mental exercises that force him to confront his fears, building mental toughness is essential.

One way to cultivate mental toughness is through controlled exposure to discomfort. In his preparations, Jack can simulate stressful or uncomfortable situations in a safe environment. For example, he could practice enduring long periods of silence or darkness, experience outdoor camping in harsh weather, or train to stay alert during fatigue. These experiences condition the mind to remain calm when faced with actual crises, and reinforce the idea that discomfort does not equal danger.

DISCIPLINE AND CONSISTENCY

A large part of developing the Navy SEAL mindset revolves around discipline. SEALs train with a relentless commitment to their objectives, knowing that consistency is key to overcoming obstacles. In Jack's case, this means creating a routine of preparedness that includes regular physical training, mental resilience exercises, and ongoing education in survival skills.

Daily discipline—whether it's getting up early for a run, practicing problem-solving under stress, or teaching his children basic survival tasks—helps Jack foster a mentality of perseverance. Each small action builds toward an overall readiness that will serve him when the time comes to put his training to the test. Developing discipline isn't about doing grand gestures; it's about creating habits that reinforce the desired mindset over time.

In survival, routine breeds comfort. If Jack's family has a structured, well-practiced plan, they'll feel more in control, even when everything around them feels uncertain. The repetition of their drills and exercises will create a sense of familiarity and reduce fear in high-pressure situations.

ADAPTABILITY AND FLEXIBILITY

Another core aspect of the Navy SEAL mindset is adaptability. In life-or-death situations, plans rarely go perfectly. SEALs are trained to adapt quickly, adjust their strategies on the fly, and make decisions under pressure. This flexibility is something Jack must internalize as part of his mental preparation.

In a survival scenario, there will be constant change—whether it's environmental factors, unforeseen obstacles, or new threats emerging. Jack's ability to adapt to these changes without losing focus or becoming overwhelmed will define his success. Learning to stay calm and make quick decisions in the face of chaos is an integral part of developing mental resilience.

One method Jack can practice is improvisation. He can challenge himself and his family to create solutions to unexpected problems without warning. For example, how would they react if their generator failed? What would they do if their water supply was suddenly compromised? By training the mind to respond creatively to adversity, Jack ensures that his mental flexibility remains sharp.

Controlling Fear and Panic

Fear is one of the greatest enemies in a crisis, but SEALs are trained to face their fears head-on and use it as fuel for action. The Navy SEAL mindset doesn't ignore fear; rather, it acknowledges fear as a natural human emotion and then channels it into productive responses. For Jack, this means understanding that feeling afraid during a crisis is normal—but it's what he does with that fear that will determine his survival.

A practical way for Jack to practice controlling fear is through breathing exercises and meditation techniques. Navy SEALs often use techniques like box breathing—a method of inhaling for four seconds, holding for four, exhaling for four, and holding again for four. This rhythmic breathing technique calms the mind, reduces the body's stress response, and allows the brain to think clearly. By practicing this regularly, Jack can help his body and mind remain composed during actual moments of fear.

Another key is mental visualization. Jack can use guided visualizations where he imagines worst-case scenarios and mentally walks through how he would handle each step. This not only prepares him mentally but also desensitizes him to the initial panic that might arise in a real-life crisis. When Jack has already "seen" himself managing a situation in his mind, it becomes easier to handle when it occurs in reality.

Embracing a "Never Quit" Attitude

At the core of the Navy SEAL mindset is the "never quit" attitude. SEALs are ingrained with the belief that, no matter how bad things get, they can always keep going. This relentless perseverance is what separates those who survive from those who falter in a crisis.

For Jack, adopting this unbreakable spirit means committing to a mindset where quitting is not an option. It's about knowing that no matter how difficult the situation becomes—whether it's a lack of resources, injury, or overwhelming fatigue—he will find a way to survive. This is especially important for keeping his family motivated and focused on survival. If Jack can maintain this "never quit" attitude, it will ripple out to his family, giving them the courage and determination to follow his lead.

One way to develop this mentality is through physical endurance challenges, such as long-distance hikes, timed challenges, or physical stress tests. These experiences teach Jack that his body and mind are capable of far more than he may believe, reinforcing the idea that there's always more strength and resilience to tap into when things seem impossible.

Focus on the Mission

In any crisis, the ability to remain focused on the mission is critical. The Navy SEAL mindset teaches that, even when everything around you is falling apart, staying focused on the objective will guide you through. For Jack, his mission is clear: to protect and provide for his family during a crisis. By keeping this goal at the forefront of his mind, he can avoid being distracted by fear, frustration, or external chaos.

This focus also applies to breaking down the mission into smaller, manageable tasks. Instead of worrying about the enormity of a long-term crisis, Jack can focus on immediate, actionable steps—whether it's ensuring the water supply is safe, rotating food stores, or checking the perimeter defenses. By keeping his attention on what he can control, Jack can maintain clarity of thought and effective action.

Preparing Your Family for High-Stress Scenarios

In times of crisis, having a well-prepared family is not just about having physical supplies or security measures in place. It's also about ensuring that each family member is mentally equipped to handle high-stress scenarios. Jack understands that survival isn't just about his own ability to stay calm and resilient but about preparing his entire family to face unpredictable challenges together. This preparation is vital in preventing panic, ensuring clear communication, and fostering unity during tough times.

Preparing a family for high-stress situations means addressing emotional, psychological, and practical concerns in advance. It requires a holistic approach that incorporates training, open communication, and setting expectations for various crisis situations.

The Importance of Family Training

When it comes to survival, everyone in the family has a role to play. Whether it's taking charge of specific tasks or simply knowing how to stay calm and follow instructions, family training is essential to ensure that each member is confident in their abilities. Training together helps foster a sense of responsibility and readiness while minimizing confusion in high-stress situations.

For Jack, training his family doesn't need to involve military-level drills, but it does require regular practice and simulations of possible scenarios. Drills should be practical, covering skills like basic first aid, how to use communication devices, securing entry points, or how to react in case of fire or evacuation. By practicing together, the family becomes familiar with what to do in various crises, minimizing hesitation when faced with real stressors.

Involving children in these exercises is especially important. While they may not be able to perform all tasks, teaching them age-appropriate skills, such as where to go during an emergency or how to call for help, builds their confidence. Jack should also help them understand the significance of teamwork, focusing on how everyone's contribution helps keep the family safe.

Teaching Stress Management Techniques

Surviving high-stress situations often hinges on the ability to remain calm and make rational decisions under pressure. Jack knows that stress is inevitable, especially when facing a prolonged crisis, but the way his family handles stress can make all the difference.

One effective method is to teach breathing exercises and mindfulness techniques to help manage anxiety in real time. Deep breathing, for example, can help regulate the body's response to stress, slowing the heart rate and allowing for clearer thinking. Jack can lead his family in practicing simple breathing techniques like box breathing or diaphragmatic breathing, which can quickly calm the mind and body in moments of fear or overwhelm.

Incorporating stress-relief activities into the family's routine can also be beneficial. Whether it's going for daily walks, doing simple exercises together, or practicing meditation, these activities can help regulate stress over the long term and provide a healthy outlet during times of crisis. For Jack, creating a calm, stable environment before a crisis hits will help ensure his family has the mental resilience to withstand long-term stressors.

Clear and Calm Communication in High-Stress Moments

One of the most important aspects of preparing a family for high-stress scenarios is fostering clear and calm communication. When emotions run high, communication can easily break down, leading to confusion, frustration, or even danger. Jack must lead by example, maintaining a calm demeanor and ensuring his family knows how to communicate effectively during emergencies.

To do this, Jack should establish pre-agreed signals or codes that the family can use to communicate in a crisis. Whether it's a simple hand signal, a designated word, or a specific sequence of movements, these codes allow the family to convey important information quickly and discreetly if verbal communication isn't possible.

In addition to having signals, Jack should teach his family the importance of active listening and staying focused on the task at hand. During an emergency, distractions can be dangerous, so practicing listening and responding calmly to instructions is key. Children, in particular, may need help developing the discipline to follow directions without getting distracted by fear or panic.

Jack should also encourage open and honest communication after drills or real-life events. By discussing what went well and what didn't, the family can identify areas for improvement and learn from each experience, strengthening their overall resilience for the future.

Preparing for Emotional Responses

In high-stress situations, people respond emotionally in different ways. Some may shut down, while others may become overwhelmed with fear, anger, or frustration. Jack knows that preparing his family for these emotional responses is just as important as preparing them physically.

To help his family process emotions during a crisis, Jack can introduce emotional resilience exercises that allow them to express their feelings in healthy ways. Journaling, for example, can be a useful tool for both adults and children to release their thoughts and feelings, especially when there's no immediate solution to a crisis.

Additionally, role-playing exercises can help family members understand their emotional responses in a safe environment. By simulating various stressful scenarios, Jack can observe how each member reacts and provide guidance on managing emotions constructively. This can include learning how to self-soothe by engaging in calming activities or simply practicing how to respond to fear without becoming overwhelmed.

Jack should also teach the family to recognize emotional cues in each other. When they can see that a family member is beginning to feel stressed or scared, they can step in with reassurance or help them focus on practical tasks to redirect their energy. Fostering empathy and emotional support within the family will make it easier to face adversity together.

Assigning Roles and Responsibilities

A crucial part of preparing for high-stress scenarios is ensuring that each family member knows their role and responsibilities. Assigning specific tasks can reduce feelings of helplessness, as everyone will have something to focus on. When each person knows their role, they can work together more efficiently, making the situation more manageable for the entire family.

Jack should designate roles based on individual strengths and abilities. For example, one family member could be responsible for managing communication, while another might be in charge of preparing food or gathering supplies. Younger children, even if they can't take on major responsibilities, can still contribute by helping with simple tasks like fetching items or keeping track of younger siblings.

By assigning roles in advance, Jack ensures that his family can move into action quickly during a crisis, with minimal confusion or debate about who is responsible for what. This also instills a sense of purpose and responsibility in each family member, fostering teamwork and unity under pressure.

Preparing for the Long Term

Jack's family must also be prepared for the possibility of long-term crises that require sustained mental resilience. While short-term high-stress situations may be manageable with immediate actions, long-term scenarios such as extended isolation or food shortages can have a cumulative effect on stress levels.

In these cases, Jack should encourage his family to maintain routines that provide structure and stability. Daily tasks, even simple ones like cleaning or exercising, can help create a sense of normalcy and reduce feelings of chaos. Setting goals, even small ones, will give the family something to focus on and a sense of achievement.

Additionally, Jack can introduce coping mechanisms for long-term stress, such as creating art projects, engaging in hobbies, or learning new skills. These activities serve as a positive distraction and provide mental stimulation, preventing boredom and frustration from taking hold.

Exercises for Building Mental Fortitude

Mental fortitude is one of the most crucial traits for survival in high-stress and prolonged crises. It's not enough to be physically prepared; the ability to remain calm, focused, and resilient in the face of adversity is what ensures long-term survival. For Jack and his family, building mental fortitude means engaging in deliberate exercises that challenge their minds to withstand pressure, manage stress, and continue to function optimally, even under extreme conditions. Developing this strength will make all the difference when external circumstances push them to their limits.

This section focuses on practical exercises that Jack can incorporate into his family's preparedness routine, helping each member of the family build mental resilience and the ability to adapt to tough situations.

Stress Exposure Training

Stress exposure training is a method used by elite military units, like the Navy SEALs, to desensitize individuals to the physiological effects of stress. It's about intentionally putting yourself in uncomfortable or high-pressure situations so that your body and mind learn how to respond without panicking.

Jack can integrate stress exposure into his family's routine by simulating crisis scenarios. These could include mock drills where the family practices emergency protocols under timed conditions, forcing them to respond quickly and calmly. For example, simulating a sudden power outage or a home invasion drill can help the family learn how to react in a controlled manner without succumbing to panic.

When introducing this exercise, Jack should begin with low-intensity scenarios and gradually increase the difficulty as the family grows more accustomed to handling stress. The idea is to train the mind to remain clear and focused, even when the situation becomes more demanding.

Another variation of stress exposure is practicing physical endurance in difficult conditions. This could mean going for long hikes or engaging in physical activities that challenge the family's stamina, all while incorporating problem-solving elements like navigating unfamiliar terrain or setting up camp under pressure. These activities mimic real-world survival situations where fatigue, hunger, and stress will likely be part of the equation.

Mental Visualization and Guided Imagery

Visualization techniques are used by professional athletes, military personnel, and top performers in high-stakes fields to prepare their minds for success. In survival situations, visualizing potential scenarios and mentally rehearsing how to respond can enhance preparedness, reduce fear, and improve confidence.

For Jack, teaching his family mental visualization is a valuable way to help them prepare for different crises. The exercise involves having each family member close their eyes and walk through various stressful situations in their minds, focusing on how they would remain calm, handle obstacles, and take the necessary actions. For instance, Jack can guide them through visualizing what they would do during a natural disaster—first hearing the warning, then moving through each step to secure the home, gather supplies, and protect each other.

The key to effective visualization is to engage all the senses. Jack should encourage his family to imagine not just what they would see, but also what they would hear, smell, and feel in that moment. The more detailed the visualization, the more mentally prepared the family will feel when faced with the real thing.

Guided imagery is another useful tool. Jack can create specific mental images of positive outcomes after a crisis. This helps shift the mindset from fear and anxiety to confidence and control. By visualizing success, the family builds the mental strength to approach problems with an optimistic and solutions-oriented mindset.

Controlled Breathing Techniques

Breathing exercises are simple but incredibly effective tools for building mental fortitude, especially in stressful situations. When the body encounters stress, the fight-or-flight response is triggered, leading to increased heart rate, shallow breathing, and heightened anxiety. Learning to control breathing is a way to manage the body's physical response to stress, allowing the mind to stay calm and make rational decisions.

One of the most common and effective techniques is box breathing, used by Navy SEALs to regulate their breathing under extreme conditions. Jack can practice this technique with his family by following these steps:

- Inhale for 4 seconds.
- Hold the breath for 4 seconds.
- Exhale for 4 seconds.
- Hold again for 4 seconds.

Repeating this cycle helps calm the nervous system and brings focus back to the present moment. Jack can integrate this practice into the family's daily routine or use it as a quick tool during drills when emotions start to rise.

Additionally, diaphragmatic breathing (deep belly breathing) helps to slow down the body's response to stress. This exercise involves inhaling deeply into the abdomen rather than taking shallow breaths into the chest. Practicing this type of breathing can also increase oxygen flow to the brain, improving cognitive function in high-pressure situations.

Mental Toughness Challenges

Building mental fortitude requires pushing beyond the mind's perceived limits. Mental toughness challenges are designed to help individuals confront discomfort and break through psychological barriers that tell them to stop when things get hard. Jack can introduce these challenges as part of the family's preparedness training.

These challenges could involve completing physically demanding tasks—like running a certain distance, carrying heavy items, or hiking uphill—while managing mental stressors such as time constraints or simulated threats. The idea is to teach the family that their minds can often endure more than they think, and that giving up is not an option.

During these challenges, Jack should emphasize positive self-talk, another key component of mental resilience. Encouraging the family to replace negative thoughts like "I can't do this" with positive affirmations like "I've got this" helps shift their mindset from defeat to determination. Over time, these mental toughness challenges will condition the family to face difficulties head-on and keep going, even when the situation seems overwhelming.

Cognitive Flexibility Training

Cognitive flexibility is the ability to adapt and shift thinking in response to changing circumstances. In survival situations, rigidity can be dangerous—being able to quickly adjust strategies when plans don't go as expected is a crucial skill for staying alive.

To build cognitive flexibility, Jack can engage his family in exercises that challenge their problem-solving abilities under pressure. These could be puzzle-solving activities, navigating unfamiliar environments with limited resources, or participating in timed drills that require them to think on their feet. The goal is to simulate the type of unpredictability they might face during a real crisis and help them develop the mental agility to adjust accordingly.

Jack could also introduce brain games or mental exercises that improve cognitive function, like memory games, strategy puzzles, or problem-solving activities. These not only sharpen the mind but also teach the family how to approach complex challenges from multiple angles, an essential skill when resources are scarce, and quick thinking is required.

Emotional Regulation Exercises

Finally, mental fortitude includes the ability to regulate emotions under pressure. In high-stress situations, emotions like fear, anger, or frustration can cloud judgment and lead to poor decisions. Teaching the family how to process and regulate emotions is essential for building long-term mental resilience.

One exercise Jack can introduce is emotional journaling, where each family member writes about their emotions after participating in a drill or during stressful moments in real life. This exercise helps them become more aware of their emotional responses and identify patterns of behavior. Recognizing these patterns allows them to control their emotions better in the future, especially when high stakes are involved.

Additionally, practicing gratitude can help shift focus away from negative emotions and maintain a positive outlook during difficult times. Each family member could list things they're grateful for, even during tough drills or challenging moments. This mindset shift helps foster resilience and boosts morale, which is crucial in long-term crises.

Managing Long-Term Isolation and Confined Spaces

In any long-term survival scenario, one of the most difficult aspects to manage is isolation, particularly when confined to a limited space for an extended period. For Jack and his family, being mentally prepared to endure such a situation is just as important as having sufficient food and water. Isolation and confinement bring a unique set of psychological challenges, including cabin fever, anxiety, boredom, and feelings of helplessness. Without proper preparation, these factors can deteriorate the morale and mental health of even the strongest individuals.

Navy SEALs undergo rigorous training to manage long-term isolation and confined spaces during missions, and many of their strategies can be adapted to civilian life. By preparing in advance and implementing a structured approach to isolation, Jack can help his family navigate the psychological difficulties of confined living, maintain their resilience, and protect their mental well-being.

Creating a Routine for Stability

When normal life is disrupted, such as during a prolonged crisis where families must stay indoors for weeks or months, creating a structured routine becomes critical. A predictable routine gives a sense of control and purpose, reducing anxiety and helping each family member maintain a sense of normalcy. Without a routine, time can feel disjointed and overwhelming, leading to feelings of confusion or despair.

Jack can set up a daily schedule that includes regular times for meals, hygiene, exercise, and rest. For example, morning routines could focus on physical activity, followed by a shared family breakfast, while afternoons might include learning new skills or engaging in creative activities. The key is consistency. Having a plan for each day—even if it's a simple one—can help prevent boredom and restlessness from taking hold.

Involving the family in the creation of the routine also gives them a sense of ownership and helps ensure that everyone is on the same page. Additionally, including time for individual solitude within the routine can be important, as it allows each person to have space to reflect, decompress, and reset mentally.

Physical and Mental Exercises

Maintaining both physical and mental activity is essential during isolation. Without physical exertion, the body weakens, and the mind can become lethargic. This can worsen the effects of confinement. For Jack, including daily exercise routines not only helps keep the family fit and healthy but also releases endorphins, which naturally boost mood and reduce stress.

Physical activities could be simple, such as bodyweight exercises like push-ups, sit-ups, or stretching routines that can be done in a confined space. Jack can also incorporate fun, active games like obstacle courses for the children or challenge-based exercises that involve teamwork.

On the mental side, it's equally important to engage in activities that stimulate the brain. These might include puzzles, strategy games, or learning new skills, such as knitting, coding, or playing a musical instrument. Keeping the brain active helps prevent boredom and ensures that each family member remains mentally sharp and adaptable to the long-term situation.

Managing Cabin Fever

Cabin fever is a well-known psychological phenomenon that arises when people are stuck in a confined space for too long, with little exposure to the outside world. Symptoms often include irritability, restlessness, difficulty concentrating, and mood swings. For Jack and his family, it's critical to recognize the signs early and take action to prevent cabin fever from taking over.

One effective strategy is to stay connected to nature in any way possible. Even if confined to a home, Jack can encourage his family to spend time near windows, taking in natural light and fresh air. If the house has a garden, patio, or balcony, spending time outdoors can provide a significant mental boost. When going outside is not an option, Jack can bring nature indoors by incorporating plants or simulating natural sounds, such as birdsong or rainfall, to create a more pleasant and soothing atmosphere.

Another way to combat cabin fever is by rotating activities and creating a sense of variety within the confined space. Rearranging furniture, changing the family's view by using different rooms for different activities, or even setting up themed nights (such as movie night or game night) can help break the monotony of confinement.

Staying Social in Isolation

While physical isolation is a given in many survival scenarios, social isolation should be minimized as much as possible. Human beings are naturally social creatures, and long-term isolation without meaningful interaction can lead to depression and other mental health challenges.

Jack should make sure that his family stays socially connected, both with each other and, when possible, with friends and extended family outside the home. Regular family meetings where everyone can share their thoughts, feelings, and concerns in a safe, open environment are critical. These meetings also provide an opportunity to address any tensions or conflicts that may arise from living in close quarters.

If communication with the outside world is available, maintaining virtual connections with loved ones through phone calls, video chats, or online messaging can help alleviate feelings of isolation. For children, it can be particularly important to stay connected with their friends, as this helps them maintain a sense of normalcy and social engagement, even in isolation.

Coping with Loneliness and Anxiety

In any long-term isolation scenario, loneliness and anxiety are common emotions that each family member may experience. Jack's role is to ensure that these feelings don't become overwhelming. To do this, he can introduce relaxation techniques, such as meditation or deep breathing exercises, to help his family manage anxiety.

Meditation can be a powerful tool for coping with isolation, as it encourages mindfulness and helps individuals stay grounded in the present moment. Practicing even a few minutes of meditation each day can reduce stress and promote mental clarity. Jack can lead his family in guided meditations, using breathing exercises to calm the mind and reduce feelings of unease.

In addition, Jack should foster an environment of emotional support where each family member feels comfortable expressing their emotions without judgment. When emotions like sadness, frustration, or fear arise, they should be acknowledged and discussed openly. This reduces the stigma of negative feelings and ensures that no one feels alone in their experience.

Creating a Positive Environment

Finally, maintaining positivity within the confined space is essential for long-term resilience. The environment should be conducive to both productivity and relaxation, with designated areas for work, play, and rest. Jack can make small changes to improve the mood of the space, such as adding colorful decorations, playing uplifting music, or introducing small rewards and celebrations for family achievements, like completing a task or learning a new skill.

Creating a fun atmosphere doesn't negate the seriousness of a crisis—it strengthens mental health by allowing moments of joy and laughter even in difficult times. For Jack, keeping spirits high is about balance: ensuring that his family is prepared, engaged, and supported, while also allowing room for humor and lightheartedness.

Keeping Spirits High: Motivation in a Crisis

In a prolonged crisis, when the initial adrenaline has worn off, keeping spirits high becomes one of the most challenging but essential aspects of survival. Motivation isn't just about keeping yourself physically active or mentally alert; it's about maintaining hope, purpose, and a sense of forward momentum even in the face of overwhelming obstacles. For Jack, ensuring that his family stays motivated during a crisis is key to their collective resilience. This requires conscious effort, proactive strategies, and a deep understanding of what fuels individual and group morale.

Maintaining high spirits is not merely a matter of positive thinking—it's about creating an environment where every family member feels connected to a sense of purpose, knows their value, and has hope for the future. Understanding how to cultivate this mindset is crucial for survival, especially during long-term crises where isolation, fear, and stress can easily lead to hopelessness and demotivation.

The Role of Leadership in Sustaining Morale

One of the first aspects of keeping spirits high is understanding the role of leadership. Jack, as the head of his family, serves as the emotional and motivational anchor during a crisis. His attitude, actions, and emotional resilience set the tone for the rest of the family. Leadership during a crisis isn't just about making decisions and ensuring physical safety; it's about managing the emotional climate of the household.

Jack must exhibit calm and strength in the face of adversity, modeling behavior that shows confidence and adaptability. His ability to remain composed during difficult times will help reassure his family and prevent panic from taking over. Leadership also means being open to the emotional needs of each family member, providing support, and creating space for their concerns and fears to be expressed without judgment.

Moreover, Jack should recognize when the family's morale is dipping and take proactive steps to address it. Whether through motivational talks, offering encouragement, or simply leading by example, Jack's leadership can either be the glue that holds the family together or the key to ensuring they don't lose hope.

Finding Purpose in Daily Activities

One of the most effective ways to maintain motivation during a crisis is by instilling a sense of purpose in daily activities. Without a sense of purpose, the days can blend into each other, creating a feeling of stagnation and futility. However, when Jack and his family can attach meaning to their tasks—whether big or small—it keeps them engaged and focused.

For example, assigning each family member a specific role in the household's survival plan creates a sense of responsibility and accomplishment. Whether it's overseeing the water supply, managing food storage, or being in charge of maintaining communication devices, these roles give each person a tangible way to contribute to the family's survival. Knowing that they are essential to the collective well-being helps maintain high spirits, even during the toughest times.

In addition, Jack can introduce short-term goals within the larger framework of survival. These goals could be as simple as organizing supplies, improving personal fitness, or learning a new skill. Having these small milestones provides a sense of achievement and progress, which keeps motivation alive. It shifts the focus from merely surviving to thriving under the circumstances, reinforcing the idea that the family is still moving forward, despite the crisis.

Recognizing and Celebrating Small Wins

Another effective way to keep spirits high is by recognizing and celebrating small wins. These moments of success—no matter how minor—should be acknowledged and appreciated. Surviving one more day, successfully completing a challenging task, or overcoming a stressful situation are all worthy of recognition.

Jack should make it a habit to point out these moments, ensuring that the family feels a sense of pride and accomplishment. Celebrations don't have to be elaborate or formal; they can be as simple as taking a break to enjoy a special treat, playing a family game, or simply saying words of encouragement. These small rituals of celebration can lift the family's mood and provide a much-needed break from the constant stress of survival.

Recognizing achievements helps shift the focus away from what the family lacks and toward what they have accomplished together. It builds a narrative of progress and resilience, which is essential for maintaining motivation in a crisis.

Maintaining Emotional Connection

During long-term crises, isolation can lead to emotional disconnect, especially when everyone is focused on survival tasks. Maintaining emotional connection within the family is critical to keeping spirits high. This involves being emotionally present and engaged with each family member.

Jack should regularly check in with his family, offering opportunities to talk about their feelings and experiences. This not only fosters emotional connection but also provides a safe space to release tension and alleviate stress. Sometimes, the simple act of listening can be a powerful tool in maintaining motivation, as it reinforces the feeling that each family member is cared for and valued.

Additionally, Jack can encourage activities that foster emotional bonding. These could include storytelling, playing games, or even sharing memories from before the crisis. By fostering a sense of unity and togetherness, Jack can help his family feel more grounded, reducing feelings of isolation and strengthening their collective motivation.

Managing Setbacks with Optimism

In any crisis, setbacks are inevitable. Whether it's an unexpected loss of supplies, a break-down in communication, or an illness, these challenges can easily undermine morale. However, how these setbacks are managed will determine whether they erode motivation or become opportunities for growth.

Jack should lead his family in approaching setbacks with realistic optimism. This means acknowledging the difficulty of the situation without sugarcoating it but also focusing on solutions and moving forward. For example, if the family loses a critical resource, Jack can guide them through the problem-solving process, encouraging creativity and adaptability.

It's essential that setbacks are framed as learning experiences rather than failures. By shifting the narrative, Jack can help his family see each obstacle as something they can overcome together, reinforcing their belief in their own resilience. This perspective is crucial in keeping spirits high, as it prevents setbacks from becoming the final blow to motivation.

Incorporating Moments of Joy

Despite the gravity of a crisis, it's important to incorporate moments of joy and laughter into daily life. These moments provide a break from stress, allowing the family to reset and refocus. Jack can create opportunities for fun activities, whether it's playing board games, watching a movie, or telling jokes to lighten the mood.

Creating a balance between serious survival tasks and lighthearted moments is essential. Laughter, in particular, is a powerful antidote to stress and can help release tension in the household. It's not about ignoring the seriousness of the situation but about allowing the family to recharge their emotional batteries through shared enjoyment.

By keeping spirits high with moments of joy, Jack helps his family remember that even in the darkest times, there are reasons to smile, laugh, and feel hopeful. These moments act as a mental and emotional reset, giving everyone the energy to keep going, even when the challenges seem insurmountable.

CHAPTER 6

EMERGENCY MEDICINE AND HEALTH SELF-SUFFICIENCY

- -

Building a Complete Home First Aid Kit

One of the most fundamental steps toward ensuring your family's safety during a crisis is building a comprehensive home first aid kit. This kit is not just a collection of bandages and antiseptics; it is a lifeline that equips you to handle a wide range of injuries, from minor cuts to more severe traumas, when professional medical assistance may not be available. Jack understands the importance of being fully prepared for any situation, and having a well-stocked first aid kit is a cornerstone of that preparation. This chapter will walk you through the key elements necessary to build a complete and effective home first aid kit, ensuring you and your family are ready for whatever emergencies may arise.

Understanding the Scope of Your First Aid Kit

Before you begin gathering supplies, it's important to understand the scope and purpose of your first aid kit. This isn't a kit for everyday scrapes or a quick trip to the park; it's a robust and versatile medical toolkit designed to support your family's health and safety during an extended crisis. Whether it's treating a deep cut, managing a burn, or administering CPR, your first aid kit should provide the tools needed for various emergencies when medical help is unavailable.

To achieve this, Jack needs to consider the types of injuries that are most likely to occur during the specific crises his family may face. Injuries from physical labor (such as wounds or sprains), illnesses caused by compromised sanitation, and even stress-induced conditions (such as headaches or stomachaches) should all be accounted for. Building a kit that covers these scenarios will ensure that Jack's family has the resources necessary to handle a variety of emergencies.

Essential Items for Wound Care

The first category of supplies in any first aid kit is wound care. In a crisis, even minor wounds can become serious if not treated properly, and infections can set in quickly without the right supplies. Jack will want to stock his kit with essentials for cleaning, dressing, and protecting wounds of various types.

- Antiseptic wipes and alcohol pads are crucial for cleaning wounds before applying dressings. These should be the first line of defense to prevent infection, especially when clean water may not be available.

- Sterile gauze pads and roll bandages will help protect and cover wounds. Jack should include multiple sizes and types, ensuring there are options for both small cuts and larger abrasions or burns.

- Adhesive bandages (in multiple sizes) should be included for smaller cuts and scrapes.

- Antibiotic ointment like Neosporin or other topical antibiotics can be applied to wounds to promote healing and prevent infection.

- Medical tape is essential for securing dressings and can be used in conjunction with gauze for larger wounds that require more protection.

Additionally, Jack will want to include butterfly closures or steri-strips for closing wounds that may not require stitches but need to be kept tightly sealed.

Trauma and Emergency Care

In a survival situation, there is always the risk of more severe injuries that go beyond simple wound care. Having supplies on hand to manage traumatic injuries could make the difference between life and death. Jack's first aid kit needs to include items that are suitable for addressing these more serious conditions.

- Tourniquets are essential for stopping severe bleeding, especially in situations where immediate medical attention isn't possible. Jack should familiarize himself and his family with proper tourniquet application, as improper use can cause additional harm.

- Hemostatic dressings or clotting agents, such as QuickClot, are useful in stopping heavy bleeding and should be included in the kit. These specialized items are designed to control severe blood loss and should be readily accessible.

- Splints or SAM splints will be invaluable for stabilizing broken or sprained limbs. While improvisation is possible in a pinch, having proper splinting materials ensures better support and faster recovery.

- CPR masks should also be part of the kit to protect both the rescuer and the patient in case of respiratory emergencies. Jack can include an AED (Automated External Defibrillator) if possible, though it's an advanced item that might not be feasible for every household.

Managing Pain and Inflammation

No first aid kit is complete without medications for managing pain, inflammation, and fever. While Jack cannot stockpile prescription drugs without consulting a medical professional, he can gather over-the-counter (OTC) medications that address a wide range of ailments.

- Ibuprofen (Advil) or acetaminophen (Tylenol) are must-haves for managing pain, reducing fever, and controlling inflammation. Both are commonly available, and Jack should ensure he has enough for his family to last through an extended crisis.

- Aspirin can be included, not only for pain relief but also because it can be administered during a suspected heart attack, potentially saving a life in the critical moments before professional help arrives.

- Antihistamines such as Benadryl are essential for treating allergic reactions, which can be life-threatening if severe. Jack should also include epinephrine auto-injectors (such as an EpiPen) if anyone in the family has a history of severe allergies.

Specialty Items for Specific Needs

Depending on the specific health needs of his family, Jack may need to include specialty items in his first aid kit. For instance, if anyone in the family has chronic conditions, Jack should ensure that their medical supplies—whether it's insulin for diabetes or an inhaler for asthma—are readily available and stored safely.

It's also wise to consider the possibility of eye injuries or irritations, especially in dusty or polluted environments. Jack can include eye wash solution or sterile saline to flush out debris or chemicals from the eyes.

Natural Remedies and Herbal Solutions

Jack's first aid kit should not rely solely on pharmaceutical solutions; incorporating natural and herbal remedies can provide an additional layer of health support. There may come a time when traditional medications are no longer available, so knowing how to use natural alternatives will ensure the family has ongoing access to healing options.

- Tea tree oil and lavender oil are both excellent natural antiseptics that can be applied to wounds or used to treat skin irritations.

- Aloe vera gel is highly effective for treating burns, cuts, and other skin conditions.

- Arnica cream can be used for bruising and muscle pain, offering relief without the need for OTC painkillers.

- Activated charcoal can be used in cases of poisoning, although Jack should also be cautious and well-informed before administering it, as it isn't appropriate for all types of poisons.

Keeping Everything Organized and Accessible

One of the most important aspects of a first aid kit is organization. In an emergency, Jack won't have time to rummage through a disorganized kit. He needs a system that allows him to quickly locate and access the supplies he needs.

Jack can use a tiered system to categorize items based on urgency and type. For example, wound care supplies could be grouped together, while trauma supplies could be in a separate, clearly labeled section. Color-coded bags or pouches can make organization easier and allow for quick identification of key items.

Additionally, Jack should ensure that his family knows where the first aid kit is stored and how to use its contents. Holding practice sessions to familiarize everyone with the supplies and their proper usage will prevent confusion and hesitation during a real emergency.

Treating Common Ailments Without External Help

In any extended crisis or survival situation, access to medical professionals or healthcare facilities may be limited, if not entirely unavailable. This reality places the responsibility of treating common ailments squarely on the shoulders of individuals and families. For Jack and his family, learning how to manage everyday health issues without external assistance is a critical skill. While serious injuries or illnesses will always require medical expertise when possible, many common conditions can be addressed with basic knowledge, a well-prepared first aid kit, and some practical home remedies. In this section, we will explore how Jack can confidently handle common ailments like headaches, colds, digestive issues, and minor infections, using the resources at hand.

Managing Headaches and Migraines

Headaches are one of the most frequent ailments people encounter, and they can range from mild discomfort to debilitating migraines. In a survival situation, stress, dehydration, lack of sleep, or poor nutrition can all trigger headaches, making them even more common. While over-the-counter painkillers like ibuprofen or acetaminophen should always be included in Jack's first aid kit, it's also important to have alternative strategies for managing headaches without medication, in case supplies run low.

One effective approach is ensuring proper hydration. Dehydration is a major cause of headaches, and in a crisis, access to clean drinking water might be limited. Jack should make hydration a priority for his family, encouraging everyone to drink regularly and avoid caffeinated or sugary drinks that may exacerbate dehydration. Additionally, applying a cold compress or ice pack to the forehead or neck can provide relief from tension headaches by constricting blood vessels and reducing inflammation.

For migraines, stress management techniques like deep breathing exercises or meditation can be useful. Migraines often have triggers such as stress, lack of sleep, or bright lights, so identifying and avoiding these triggers is key to prevention. Jack should also explore herbal remedies like peppermint oil or lavender oil, which can be applied to the temples to help alleviate symptoms naturally.

Treating Cold and Flu Symptoms

In the event of a prolonged crisis, it is almost inevitable that someone in Jack's household will catch a cold or the flu. With no access to over-the-counter medications like cold tablets or cough syrups, understanding how to treat cold and flu symptoms using common supplies and home remedies becomes essential.

First, ensuring proper rest and hydration is the foundation of recovery from any viral illness. Jack should encourage his family members to rest as much as possible, as overexertion can prolong illness and lead to complications. Keeping everyone hydrated with water, herbal teas, or broths will also help soothe sore throats and loosen congestion.

Natural remedies, such as a saltwater gargle, can be used to ease throat pain and reduce inflammation. Similarly, steam inhalation—using a bowl of hot water with eucalyptus oil or a similar essential oil—can help open up blocked nasal passages and relieve sinus pressure. If fever is present, Jack can utilize cool compresses to bring down body temperature, while warm teas made from ginger or chamomile may help to boost the immune system and fight off the infection.

Addressing Digestive Issues

Stomachaches, indigestion, diarrhea, and constipation are common problems that can arise during a crisis, especially when food options are limited or when stress is high. Jack should know how to treat these issues without relying on medications that may not be available.

For indigestion or heartburn, natural remedies like baking soda mixed with water can neutralize stomach acid and provide quick relief. Chewing ginger or drinking ginger tea is also highly effective in soothing an upset stomach and reducing nausea. For diarrhea, which can lead to dangerous dehydration if not addressed, Jack can prepare a simple oral rehydration solution by mixing water, salt, and sugar. This solution will help replenish lost fluids and electrolytes. He should also keep foods like bananas, rice, applesauce, and toast (the BRAT diet) on hand, as these are easy to digest and can help firm up stools.

For constipation, encouraging plenty of water intake and adding fiber-rich foods to meals will stimulate bowel movements. If fiber sources are limited, Jack can use prunes or flaxseed as natural laxatives. Herbal teas made from senna or peppermint may also help relieve constipation naturally.

Handling Minor Skin Infections and Irritations

Minor infections such as cuts, scrapes, and rashes are common, especially when cleanliness and sanitation may be compromised. Treating these quickly and effectively will prevent them from becoming serious problems.

The first step in treating any minor wound is cleaning it thoroughly with clean water or antiseptic solution. Once the area is clean, applying an antibiotic ointment or a natural remedy like honey (which has antibacterial properties) can help promote healing. For more persistent infections, garlic is a powerful natural antibiotic that can be crushed and applied to the skin as a poultice.

For rashes or skin irritations caused by allergens or environmental factors, Jack can turn to natural remedies like aloe vera or oatmeal baths to soothe inflammation. Aloe vera is especially effective at calming irritated skin, while an oatmeal bath can help reduce itching and discomfort.

Dealing with Muscle Aches and Sprains

During a survival scenario, physical labor—such as chopping wood, hauling water, or building fortifications—may result in muscle strains, sprains, and general body aches. Knowing how to manage these issues without access to medical professionals is crucial for maintaining the family's physical strength and capability.

For muscle aches, Jack can use the RICE method: Rest, Ice, Compression, and Elevation. Resting the injured area prevents further damage, while applying ice reduces inflammation. Compression with a bandage and elevating the limb can help control swelling. Including a heating pad or warm compress in his first aid kit can also soothe sore muscles once the swelling has gone down.

For natural remedies, arnica cream is highly effective for treating bruises and muscle pain. If arnica isn't available, Jack can prepare a peppermint oil rub, as peppermint has cooling and anti-inflammatory properties that can reduce pain and improve circulation to the affected area.

Managing Fever and Inflammation

Fevers are the body's natural response to infection, but they can be dangerous if they spike too high, especially in children. While medications like ibuprofen or acetaminophen are standard for reducing fever, Jack can also rely on alternative methods if these are unavailable.

A lukewarm bath can help bring down a fever, or Jack can use cold compresses applied to the forehead, wrists, and back of the neck. Herbal teas made from elderflower, catnip, or yarrow can help induce sweating, which allows the body to cool down naturally.

If inflammation is the issue—whether due to injury or illness—Jack can use natural anti-inflammatories like turmeric or ginger, which have been shown to reduce inflammation and provide relief from pain. These can be consumed in food or as tea.

Using Natural and Herbal Remedies

In times of crisis, when conventional medicine and pharmaceuticals may not be readily available, turning to natural and herbal remedies becomes essential for maintaining health and treating common ailments. These remedies, many of which have been used for centuries, provide safe, effective, and sustainable solutions for a wide range of health issues. Jack, who values resilience and preparedness, knows that building a solid foundation of knowledge on natural remedies will empower his family to handle minor health problems without relying solely on traditional medications.

Natural remedies work by harnessing the healing properties found in plants, oils, and other natural sources. From treating wounds to alleviating headaches and easing digestive troubles, herbal solutions can cover a broad spectrum of health concerns. This chapter will guide Jack in creating a well-rounded stock of natural and herbal remedies for his family's home medical kit.

The Power of Herbal Remedies: A Historical Perspective

Herbal medicine has been used by civilizations across the globe for thousands of years. Long before modern pharmaceuticals existed, people relied on plants, herbs, and natural extracts to heal wounds, fight infections, and treat illnesses. The effectiveness of many of these remedies has been supported by scientific studies, and they remain in use today as complementary or alternative treatments.

For Jack, embracing herbal remedies is about more than just practicality—it's about building self-sufficiency. By understanding the uses and benefits of various herbs, he ensures that his family has access to essential healing tools, even in a prolonged crisis where pharmaceuticals may not be an option.

Top Herbal Remedies for a Survival Situation

1. Tea Tree Oil

Tea tree oil is a must-have in Jack's natural remedy kit. This essential oil, derived from the leaves of the Melaleuca tree, has powerful antiseptic and antimicrobial properties, making it ideal for treating minor cuts, scrapes, and skin infections. Tea tree oil can be applied directly to wounds to prevent infection or diluted with water to create a cleansing solution. It's also effective in treating acne, fungal infections, and even insect bites.

2. Lavender

Known for its calming and soothing effects, lavender is not only an effective remedy for stress and anxiety, but it can also be used to treat headaches, burns, and insect bites. Lavender oil, when applied topically, can help reduce pain, inflammation, and speed up the healing process of burns. Jack can also use lavender tea to help his family relax and sleep better during stressful times.

3. Ginger

Ginger is widely recognized for its digestive benefits, but its uses extend far beyond treating nausea and indigestion. Ginger has potent anti-inflammatory and antioxidant properties, making it a valuable remedy for managing arthritis pain, reducing muscle soreness, and improving circulation. In survival situations, ginger tea can be used to soothe sore throats, ease colds, and combat motion sickness.

4. Echinacea

A powerful immune booster, echinacea is a staple for preventing and treating colds, flu, and other viral infections. Taking echinacea at the first sign of illness can help shorten its duration and reduce the severity of symptoms. In a survival scenario, Jack can either make echinacea tea or use it in tincture form to support his family's immune system during an outbreak of illness.

5. Garlic

Garlic is known as nature's antibiotic. With its antibacterial, antiviral, and antifungal properties, garlic can be used to treat infections, strengthen the immune system, and reduce inflammation. Crushed garlic can be applied directly to wounds to prevent infection, or it can be consumed raw or in food to fight off colds and respiratory infections. In a situation where antibiotics may not be available, garlic is a natural alternative that can be relied upon for its potent healing properties.

Integrating Herbal Remedies into Daily Life

For Jack, it's not just about knowing which herbs to use but also how to integrate them into daily routines to prevent illnesses and maintain health. Simple habits, such as incorporating garlic into meals, drinking ginger tea, or using lavender oil in the evenings to promote relaxation, can make a significant difference in overall well-being during a crisis.

Additionally, Jack can make use of herbal salves, balms, and poultices. For example, creating a tea tree oil and lavender balm for wound care or a ginger poultice for sore muscles are practical, hands-on ways to bring herbal remedies into his family's healthcare routine. By learning how to prepare these remedies at home, Jack increases his family's self-reliance and ability to handle health issues as they arise.

Sourcing and Growing Herbs

One of the key benefits of using natural remedies is the potential for self-sufficiency. Unlike pharmaceuticals, many herbs can be easily grown at home, making them a renewable resource. For Jack, this means that with a little planning and effort, he can cultivate a medicinal garden that will keep his family supplied with the essential herbs they need.

Starting with hardy, easy-to-grow herbs such as rosemary, thyme, and mint, Jack can expand his garden to include echinacea, lavender, and chamomile. By growing these herbs at home, he reduces his family's dependence on external supply chains, ensuring that they always have access to natural remedies. He can also dry and store herbs for future use, creating a long-lasting supply of medicinal ingredients.

Jack can also explore local foraging for wild medicinal plants. Depending on his location, herbs like plantain (useful for cuts and stings) and yarrow (known for stopping bleeding and promoting wound healing) may be readily available in the wild.

Safe Usage and Dosages

While herbal remedies can be powerful tools in Jack's home medicine cabinet, it's essential to understand that they must be used safely and appropriately. Just because something is natural doesn't mean it's free from risks. Many herbs can cause allergic reactions or interact with other medications. For example, people with ragweed allergies should avoid echinacea, while those on blood thinners should be cautious with ginger or garlic.

Jack should familiarize himself with the correct dosages for each herb and how to properly prepare them for safe use. Herbal teas and tinctures should be made with care, and topical treatments should always be tested on a small area of skin before broader application to check for sensitivity or allergic reactions. Keeping a reference guide handy that details proper dosages and potential contraindications will help Jack avoid any accidental misuse of these powerful natural remedies.

Building Herbal Knowledge

For Jack, learning about herbal medicine doesn't end with the basics. Continuous education will be key to expanding his knowledge and ability to treat a wide variety of ailments. He can study books on herbalism, attend workshops, or even consult with a local herbalist to deepen his understanding of how to use plants for healing.

Incorporating herbal remedies into daily life isn't just about treating immediate health problems; it's about cultivating a mindset of long-term health and resilience. By empowering himself with knowledge, Jack ensures that he can confidently care for his family in any crisis, even when conventional medical help is unavailable.

Emergency Medical Procedures

In a survival situation, access to professional medical care may be delayed or completely unavailable, placing the responsibility for emergency medical procedures on individuals like Jack. Being equipped with the knowledge and skills to perform essential emergency procedures can mean the difference between life and death. This chapter focuses on some of the most critical medical procedures that Jack must be familiar with to address serious injuries and health crises in the absence of immediate medical help.

The Role of Preparation and Confidence

Before diving into specific emergency medical procedures, it's essential for Jack to understand the importance of mental preparation. In high-stress situations, the ability to stay calm and confident is just as crucial as having the necessary tools. Panic can exacerbate the situation and lead to mistakes. Jack should spend time practicing key procedures in low-stress environments with his family, so that they feel more comfortable and confident performing them during a real emergency.

Confidence is built through repetition and knowledge. Jack and his family should become familiar with every item in their first aid kit and learn the basic steps of essential emergency procedures. Knowing how to respond quickly and effectively can stabilize an injury or even save a life while waiting for further assistance.

Performing CPR (Cardiopulmonary Resuscitation)

CPR (Cardiopulmonary Resuscitation) is one of the most critical emergency procedures to know. It is used when someone's heart has stopped beating or they are no longer breathing. The goal of CPR is to manually maintain blood flow to the brain and other vital organs until professional medical help arrives or until the individual starts breathing again on their own.

For Jack, learning hands-only CPR is a fundamental skill. In many survival situations, traditional CPR with mouth-to-mouth resuscitation may not be feasible or safe. Hands-only CPR focuses on chest compressions to keep blood circulating. Here's what Jack needs to remember:

- Place the heel of one hand on the center of the chest, right between the nipples. Place the other hand on top and interlock the fingers.
- Keeping his arms straight, Jack should push hard and fast, aiming for a depth of about 2 inches with each compression.
- The compression rate should be around 100-120 beats per minute, which matches the rhythm of the song "Stayin' Alive" by the Bee Gees.
- Continue compressions without stopping until professional help arrives or the person starts breathing.

In addition to CPR, Jack should consider having an AED (Automated External Defibrillator) on hand, if possible. This device can analyze the heart's rhythm and, if necessary, deliver a shock to restart it. Knowing how to use an AED correctly can significantly increase the chances of survival during a cardiac event.

Treating Severe Bleeding

Another life-threatening emergency that Jack must be prepared to handle is severe bleeding. In a survival scenario, severe cuts or injuries can quickly lead to significant blood loss, which can be fatal if not controlled immediately.

To address this, Jack should have a tourniquet in his first aid kit, as well as hemostatic dressings like QuickClot, which are designed to stop severe bleeding. Here's the basic process for treating severe bleeding:

- Apply pressure to the wound immediately using a clean cloth, gauze, or even clothing if necessary. Pressure should be firm and continuous until the bleeding slows or stops.
- If bleeding continues, Jack can use a tourniquet if the injury is on a limb. He should place the tourniquet about 2-3 inches above the wound, avoiding joints, and tighten it until the bleeding stops. Tourniquets should only be used as a last resort, as they can cause damage to the tissue if left on for too long.
- For non-tourniquet areas, using hemostatic gauze is an option. These dressings promote blood clotting and can be packed directly into the wound to help stop the bleeding.

Jack must be careful when applying a tourniquet or clotting agent. Once the bleeding is controlled, the wound should be wrapped tightly with sterile bandages to prevent further injury or infection.

Managing Airway Obstructions

Choking or airway obstructions are another medical emergency that can occur in everyday situations. Whether it's a piece of food or a foreign object, an obstructed airway can cause a person to stop breathing within minutes. Knowing how to respond to this is essential.

If a person is choking and cannot breathe, Jack should use the Heimlich maneuver:

- Stand behind the person and wrap your arms around their waist.
- Make a fist with one hand and place it just above the person's navel, below the ribcage.
- Grasp the fist with the other hand and thrust upwards and inward sharply. This should force air out of the lungs and, ideally, expel the object.
- Repeat the thrusts until the object is dislodged or the person begins breathing again.

If the Heimlich maneuver is unsuccessful, and the person loses consciousness, Jack must begin CPR to keep blood flowing and attempt to clear the airway. A family practice session of the Heimlich maneuver can help ensure everyone knows how to perform this critical lifesaving procedure.

Immobilizing Fractures and Sprains

Fractures and sprains are common injuries in survival situations, especially during physical activity or in rugged environments. Jack should be prepared to immobilize a broken limb to prevent further damage.

To immobilize a fracture, Jack should follow these steps:

- Stabilize the injured area. If a broken bone is suspected, Jack should avoid moving the limb as much as possible.
- Use a splint—either a premade SAM splint or an improvised splint using sturdy materials like wood, cardboard, or even rolled-up blankets. The splint should be long enough to support the joint above and below the fracture.
- Once the splint is in place, secure it with bandages or cloth, ensuring it is snug but not so tight that it cuts off circulation.
- If Jack is dealing with a sprain rather than a fracture, he should follow the RICE method (Rest, Ice, Compression, and Elevation) to reduce swelling and pain.

Knowing how to create improvised splints from available materials can be a crucial skill, especially if proper medical supplies aren't accessible. Items like belts, towels, or even a sturdy stick can serve as makeshift supports for injured limbs.

Treating Shock

When someone experiences trauma—whether from an injury, blood loss, or extreme stress—they can go into shock, a life-threatening condition that requires immediate attention. Shock occurs when the body is not getting enough blood flow, which can lead to organ failure if not addressed quickly.

Here's how Jack can treat shock:

- Lay the person down and elevate their legs about 12 inches, unless they have a head, neck, or back injury.
- Keep the person warm by covering them with a blanket or clothing. It's important to maintain body heat, as shock often causes the body to cool rapidly.
- Do not give them food or water. Shock can cause nausea, and consuming food or liquids may make it worse.
- If the person is unconscious or becomes unresponsive, Jack should begin CPR and seek professional medical help as soon as possible.

By learning how to manage shock, Jack will be able to stabilize someone's condition until professional medical assistance is available. Shock is a common complication of serious injuries, and recognizing the signs early is key to preventing further deterioration.

Psychological First Aid

In any crisis situation, physical health and safety are often the first priorities, but it's equally important to address the mental and emotional well-being of those involved. The psychological toll of high-stress scenarios can be overwhelming, especially during prolonged emergencies where feelings of fear, anxiety, and hopelessness can take root. For Jack, preparing to manage his family's mental and emotional health is just as critical as having a well-stocked first aid kit. Psychological First Aid (PFA) is an essential tool for helping his family cope with the emotional and psychological impacts of crises.

Psychological First Aid is not about providing therapy or counseling but rather offering immediate support and stabilization to reduce stress and foster resilience. In situations where professional mental health services may not be available, Jack can step in to offer comfort, reassurance, and practical help to his loved ones, ensuring that they can maintain a sense of hope and control, even in the most challenging circumstances.

What is Psychological First Aid?

Psychological First Aid (PFA) is an evidence-based approach designed to help individuals cope with the emotional fallout of disasters or emergencies. It involves understanding the immediate needs of those affected and offering support to prevent long-term psychological damage. The goal is to reduce initial distress, promote adaptive functioning, and instill a sense of safety and calm.

For Jack, mastering the basic principles of Psychological First Aid will enable him to:

- Provide emotional support in the face of crisis.
- Identify people who may be at risk of developing more serious mental health problems.
- Encourage positive coping strategies and promote resilience.
- Help his family process their experiences and emotions constructively.

The Core Actions of Psychological First Aid

Jack's role in offering Psychological First Aid involves a set of key actions, which can be applied immediately when his family is confronted with overwhelming stress. These actions are designed to ensure safety, foster calm, and provide a foundation for mental recovery.

1. Ensure Safety

The first priority is to make sure that everyone feels physically and emotionally safe. In a crisis, the perception of danger can heighten anxiety and fear. Jack needs to reassure his family that they are secure, whether that's by addressing concerns about home security, food supplies, or ongoing risks in the environment. This may involve practical steps, such as reinforcing home defenses or simply talking through the family's concerns and offering logical reassurance.

2. Promote Calm

In times of extreme stress, people often experience heightened emotions, such as panic, fear, or confusion. Jack can use various techniques to help his family remain calm, even when the situation feels dire. Simple breathing exercises can help regulate emotions and reduce anxiety. Jack might also lead his family through mindfulness techniques or grounding exercises to bring their focus back to the present moment, alleviating feelings of being overwhelmed.

For example, a grounding exercise might involve focusing on the five senses:

- What can you see?
- What can you hear?
- What can you touch?
- What can you smell?
- What can you taste?

These techniques redirect attention away from stress-inducing thoughts and back to immediate sensory experiences, which can promote calm.

3. Foster a Sense of Control and Self-Efficacy

A common reaction during a crisis is the feeling of helplessness or loss of control. Jack can help counteract this by giving his family members small, manageable tasks. Whether it's organizing supplies, preparing meals, or setting up defensive measures, assigning tasks allows each family member to feel they are actively contributing to the situation. This promotes a sense of control, which is critical for maintaining mental resilience.

4. Encourage Connection

Humans are social creatures, and feelings of isolation can worsen the psychological impact of a crisis. Jack should encourage his family to stay connected, whether through open communication with each other or by reaching out to others in their community if possible. Shared experiences can foster solidarity, and just talking about their fears or worries can lighten the mental burden.

5. Instill Hope

Instilling a sense of hope is perhaps one of the most important elements of Psychological First Aid. In situations where the future is uncertain, it's vital to maintain optimism and focus on positive outcomes. Jack can remind his family of past challenges they've overcome and help them focus on short-term goals to keep spirits high.

The Importance of Active Listening

One of the simplest yet most powerful tools Jack can use in offering Psychological First Aid is active listening. Often, people need to feel heard and understood before they can begin to process their emotions. By practicing active listening, Jack can provide a safe space for his family to express their feelings without judgment.

Active listening involves:

- Giving full attention to the speaker, maintaining eye contact, and offering nonverbal cues like nodding or facial expressions that indicate understanding.
- Avoiding interruptions and allowing the speaker to express themselves at their own pace.
- Reflecting back what the speaker has said, either through paraphrasing or summarizing, to show that Jack understands their concerns.

For instance, if a family member expresses fear about the future, Jack could respond with, "It sounds like you're worried about what might happen next. Let's talk about what we can control right now."

Psychological First Aid for Children

Children, in particular, are vulnerable to the emotional impact of a crisis. They may not fully understand what's happening, which can lead to feelings of confusion and fear. When providing Psychological First Aid for children, Jack must adopt a gentler approach:

- **Speak in simple terms:** Explain the situation using language that's easy for children to understand, without overwhelming them with details.
- **Offer comfort:** Physical reassurance, like a hug, can help children feel secure.
- **Maintain routines:** Whenever possible, Jack should aim to keep routines in place, as structure helps children feel more in control.
- **Encourage play:** Play is a natural way for children to process their emotions. Whether it's imaginative games or creative activities, play can help children cope with stress in a healthy way.

Long-Term Psychological Support

While Psychological First Aid is an immediate response to stress, Jack also needs to think about the long-term mental health of his family. Prolonged crises can lead to more serious issues like PTSD, depression, or anxiety disorders. It's important to monitor each family member's mental state over time and encourage self-care practices, such as journaling, exercise, or even spiritual practices if relevant.

Jack can also look for opportunities to celebrate small victories, whether it's successfully fortifying the home or maintaining a healthy food supply. These celebrations help reinforce a positive outlook and remind the family of their resilience and adaptability.

CHAPTER 7
EMERGENCY COMMUNICATION STRATEGIES

Building a Communication Network Without Electricity

In any crisis, communication becomes a vital tool for survival. Whether it's staying in touch with family, gathering information about the unfolding situation, or coordinating with neighbors, maintaining a reliable communication network can make the difference between life and death. When the power goes out, however, traditional communication systems like cell phones, internet access, and even landlines may become unusable, leaving Jack and his family vulnerable to isolation. Therefore, it's crucial for Jack to understand how to build a communication network without electricity, ensuring he and his family can stay connected during an emergency.

Why Is Communication Vital in a Crisis?

Before diving into specific solutions, it's essential to recognize why communication is so critical during an emergency. For Jack and his family, reliable communication means:

- **Receiving updates on the crisis:** Whether it's a natural disaster, civil unrest, or another form of emergency, being able to receive real-time updates can inform critical decisions, like whether to stay put or evacuate.

- **Coordinating with others:** Jack may need to communicate with neighbors, local authorities, or even rescue services. Coordinating actions, such as sharing resources or planning defense strategies, is only possible with a functioning communication network.

- **Staying connected with family:** In a crisis, family members may become separated. Having a communication plan ensures they can reunite quickly and avoid unnecessary risks.

Battery-Powered Radios: The Backbone of Crisis Communication

The most reliable and accessible option for Jack to maintain communication without electricity is a battery-powered or hand-crank radio. These devices are designed to function in off-grid situations and can receive broadcasts from local emergency services, government agencies, and weather stations.

Jack should prioritize investing in a multi-band emergency radio, which can access different frequencies, including AM, FM, and NOAA weather stations. Radios that come equipped with solar charging or hand-crank options ensure that Jack doesn't need to rely on battery supplies alone, which may become scarce over time.

Furthermore, Jack can learn how to operate shortwave radios or even consider a HAM radio setup for broader communication. HAM radios offer the unique advantage of long-range communication, allowing users to send and receive messages from across the country or even globally, depending on atmospheric conditions. With proper licensing and training, Jack could even participate in local or national amateur radio networks that coordinate disaster responses.

Walkie-Talkies and Two-Way Radios

For close-range communication within a smaller area, two-way radios or walkie-talkies are essential tools. These devices typically operate on FRS (Family Radio Service) or GMRS (General Mobile Radio Service) frequencies, allowing for short-distance communication without needing an external power source.

Jack can use two-way radios to keep in touch with family members within or around the house, and they are also useful for coordinating with nearby neighbors. These radios usually have a range of 1-3 miles, depending on the terrain and obstacles, which is more than sufficient for communication within a residential area or small community.

The benefit of using FRS or GMRS radios is their ease of use—there are no complex setups involved, and they don't require special licensing for basic use. Jack can keep multiple walkie-talkies or radios charged using solar chargers, ensuring they are always ready when needed.

Satellite Phones: The Ultimate Off-Grid Communication Tool

In some cases, relying on ground-based communication systems might not be enough. For Jack, investing in a satellite phone can provide a reliable off-grid communication solution that operates independently of local cell towers or infrastructure. Satellite phones connect directly to orbiting satellites, meaning they are unaffected by power outages, damaged cell towers, or internet blackouts.

Although satellite phones can be expensive, they offer the highest level of communication redundancy. With a satellite phone, Jack can communicate with authorities, coordinate evacuations, or request assistance from virtually anywhere in the world, as long as he has a clear view of the sky.

If Jack decides to invest in a satellite phone, he should also familiarize himself with the emergency response services offered by various satellite communication providers. Some providers offer specific emergency contact numbers, allowing users to connect with global emergency services even when local networks are down.

Solar-Powered Charging Solutions

One of the biggest challenges of maintaining a communication network without electricity is ensuring that the devices used remain charged and functional over an extended period. For Jack, this means implementing solar-powered charging systems to keep critical devices—such as radios, two-way radios, and satellite phones—operational.

Portable solar chargers and solar power banks are a crucial addition to any off-grid communication plan. These compact devices allow Jack to charge multiple gadgets, from cell phones to radios, even when the power grid is down. It's essential to choose chargers with enough power output to handle several devices simultaneously, ensuring that Jack and his family can stay connected even during extended outages.

Morse Code and Low-Tech Communication Solutions

While modern technology provides advanced options for communication, Jack should also be prepared to use low-tech solutions in extreme situations. If all else fails, traditional methods like Morse code can serve as a backup communication strategy.

Learning basic Morse code could prove invaluable in scenarios where digital communication methods are compromised. Jack can use simple tools like flashlights or mirrors to send Morse code signals over short distances. Morse code can also be transmitted via shortwave or HAM radios, allowing Jack to send messages even when voice communication is not possible.

Another low-tech option is using signal flags or smoke signals to communicate visually with nearby people. While this method is limited to short-range communication and may not always be practical, it can still serve as a useful last resort.

Establishing a Neighborhood Communication Network

In a prolonged crisis, Jack will need to coordinate not only with his family but also with his neighbors. Neighborhood communication networks are an essential part of surviving and thriving during extended emergencies, where mutual support becomes critical.

Jack can encourage his neighbors to invest in similar communication devices, such as walkie-talkies or battery-powered radios, and establish a communication protocol for emergencies. This protocol should include regular check-ins, shared frequencies, and distress signals for emergencies. For example, neighbors could agree to check in every few hours to exchange information and report any security concerns.

Additionally, creating a community radio network or a local HAM radio group can ensure that Jack and his neighbors stay informed, even if external communication systems fail. By pooling resources and knowledge, the community can create a robust communication network that helps everyone stay connected and safe.

Conclusion

In a crisis, communication is about more than just talking—it's about staying informed, staying connected, and staying alive. Building a reliable communication network without electricity requires foresight, preparation, and the right tools. For Jack, having a multi-layered communication strategy that includes battery-powered radios, walkie-talkies, satellite phones, and even low-tech options like Morse code ensures that his family can remain connected, no matter what happens. With careful planning, Jack can establish a communication network that serves as a lifeline in times of need, providing vital information, support, and coordination during any emergency.

Creating a Family Communication Plan

One of the most critical aspects of emergency preparedness is establishing a comprehensive family communication plan. In moments of crisis, when panic can spread quickly and circumstances shift unpredictably, having a clear, structured plan ensures that Jack and his family stay connected and informed, even if they're separated. A well-thought-out communication plan doesn't just provide peace of mind—it can be a lifeline that keeps everyone safe and coordinated during emergencies.

When crafting a family communication plan, Jack's primary objectives should be maintaining communication in various scenarios, ensuring everyone knows what to do in case of separation, and making sure the plan is accessible and easy to execute, even under high stress.

Why Is a Family Communication Plan Necessary?

In the chaotic aftermath of an emergency, such as a natural disaster or civil unrest, cell towers can be overwhelmed, power grids can fail, and typical methods of communication, such as phones or the internet, may be rendered useless. During these moments, family members might find themselves separated or in danger. The purpose of a family communication plan is to establish clear steps that each family member can follow, regardless of the situation.

For Jack, ensuring that his family knows how to communicate effectively under these circumstances can reduce fear, confusion, and anxiety, allowing them to make informed decisions that prioritize safety.

Key reasons for implementing a family communication plan include:

- **Rapid response to emergencies:** Time is often of the essence, and a solid plan minimizes delays in communication, enabling quicker decisions.
- **Reducing fear and uncertainty:** A predetermined plan eliminates second-guessing, helping family members feel confident that they know what to do.
- **Planning for contingencies:** The plan accounts for worst-case scenarios, ensuring communication is possible even without modern technology or when separated.

Assigning Roles and Responsibilities

The first step in creating a family communication plan is to assign specific roles and responsibilities to each family member. Jack, being the head of the family, should take the lead in establishing the communication plan and ensuring that everyone understands their part.

Key roles could include:

- **Primary communicator:** The person responsible for making initial contact and disseminating information. This could be Jack or another adult in the household.
- **Secondary communicator:** In case the primary communicator is unavailable or incapacitated, this person steps in to coordinate communication efforts.
- **Check-in coordinator:** This individual is responsible for ensuring that all family members check in at designated times or points, keeping track of each person's status.

By assigning roles, Jack ensures that communication remains organized and prevents any confusion about who should be doing what during an emergency.

Establishing Methods of Communication

A critical aspect of Jack's communication plan is determining the most reliable methods of communication during a crisis. While traditional methods like cell phones or the internet may still be the primary means of communication, the family should have backup methods that don't rely on electricity or internet infrastructure.

PRIMARY COMMUNICATION METHODS:

1. Cell Phones: If cell networks are functioning, Jack and his family should have pre-saved emergency contacts, such as one another's phone numbers, local emergency services, and any nearby family or friends.
2. Text Messaging: Even when cell towers are overwhelmed, text messages often go through when voice calls fail. Jack should ensure that everyone in the family knows

how to send a text message and understands the importance of keeping messages short and to the point during emergencies.

3. **Pre-Programmed Emergency Numbers:** Jack should make sure that all family members have pre-programmed numbers in their phones, such as those of local hospitals, police stations, or community shelters.

SECONDARY COMMUNICATION METHODS:

1. **Two-Way Radios:** These radios are an effective backup if cell service is down. Jack should make sure everyone knows how to use a two-way radio, including selecting the correct channel and using call signs for identification.

2. **Battery-Powered or Hand-Crank Radios:** These radios can be used to receive important updates from emergency services or weather stations. Jack can designate one person to monitor the radio for incoming information.

3. **Landline Telephones:** In some emergencies, landlines may still be operational even when cell networks are not. If Jack's home has a landline, it should be included in the communication plan as a potential option.

Determining Emergency Meeting Points

In case communication breaks down entirely or family members are separated, Jack should identify emergency meeting points where everyone can regroup. These meeting points should be easy to find, familiar to all family members, and located in safe areas that can be accessed even during disasters.

Jack can select:

1. **Primary Meeting Point:** This should be within or near the home. It could be the family's designated safe room or a nearby structure that is safe, such as a trusted neighbor's house.

2. **Secondary Meeting Point:** If the primary location becomes unsafe or inaccessible, a secondary location outside of the immediate area—such as a local park or community center—should be chosen.

3. **Out-of-Town Meeting Point:** For worst-case scenarios, such as widespread evacuation orders, Jack should designate an out-of-town meeting location, such as a relative's house in a neighboring city or a pre-determined safe zone.

Creating an Emergency Contact List

An emergency contact list is essential for ensuring that Jack and his family have immediate access to important phone numbers and addresses, even if their phones are down or lost. This list should include:

- **Immediate family members:** Cell numbers, work numbers, and any alternate ways to reach them.
- **Out-of-town relatives or friends:** Jack should have contact details for trusted individuals who live outside of the immediate crisis zone.
- **Local emergency services:** Fire departments, police stations, hospitals, and any community shelters should be on the list.
- **Family doctor or pediatrician:** In case of medical emergencies, it's important to have contact details for trusted healthcare providers.

Jack can laminate copies of this contact list and distribute them to every family member, ensuring they always have access to critical information, even if their phones die or paper copies are lost.

Establishing Regular Check-Ins

Jack's family should also agree on regular check-in intervals. These could be times of the day when everyone checks in with one another via phone, radio, or in person. In case of separation, these check-ins allow Jack to monitor his family's safety and determine if anyone is missing or needs assistance.

For instance, check-ins could be scheduled:

- Every two hours during an active crisis.
- At sunrise and sunset during extended periods of emergency.

Practice Makes Perfect: Conducting Drills

A family communication plan is only as effective as the family's familiarity with it. Therefore, Jack should conduct regular emergency drills to ensure that every family member knows exactly what to do in various scenarios. These drills can be simple and short, but they provide invaluable practice that can help reduce panic during a real emergency.

Setting Up Home Surveillance Systems

When it comes to fortifying your home and ensuring the safety of your family, home surveillance systems play a crucial role. In any emergency or crisis situation, having eyes on your property at all times allows you to anticipate threats, monitor suspicious activity, and act swiftly to protect what matters most. For Jack and his family, setting up an effective home surveillance system isn't just about protecting material possessions—it's about creating a secure environment where they can feel safe even in the face of uncertainty.

A robust surveillance system can offer multiple benefits, including deterring intruders, gathering evidence in the event of a breach, and giving the family peace of mind during high-stress situations. To create an effective system, Jack needs to understand what types of surveillance options are available, how to set them up effectively, and how to ensure they remain operational during a crisis.

Why Surveillance Is Essential for Home Defense

Before diving into the technical aspects of setting up a home surveillance system, it's important to understand why it's such a vital part of home defense, especially in the context of crisis scenarios. Surveillance gives Jack and his family an extra layer of protection by allowing them to detect threats before they escalate. Whether it's intruders approaching the home or suspicious activity happening at the perimeter, surveillance ensures that they are always aware of what's happening outside, reducing the chances of being caught off guard.

For Jack, knowing that he can monitor key entry points—such as doors, windows, and the garage—without leaving the safety of his home gives him a strategic advantage in a crisis. It enables him to make informed decisions about when to shelter in place, when to call for help, or when to activate additional defenses.

Choosing the Right Surveillance Equipment

To set up an effective home surveillance system, Jack needs to choose the right equipment that fits his home's unique layout, his family's security needs, and the potential challenges of an off-grid situation. There are several types of surveillance systems that Jack can consider, each with its own strengths and limitations.

WIRELESS CAMERAS

Wireless cameras are one of the most versatile and easy-to-install options for home surveillance. These cameras don't require complex wiring, making them ideal for quick setup, and they can transmit video feeds directly to Jack's phone or a computer. This makes monitoring the home possible even if Jack is away or busy with other tasks.

The key advantage of wireless cameras is that they can be placed almost anywhere around the home. For Jack, this means he can install cameras at all major entry points, including the front and back doors, windows, and even around the perimeter fence. Many wireless cameras today also come with motion-detection capabilities, sending alerts when movement is detected in a specified area.

To ensure that the cameras remain operational during a crisis, Jack should invest in battery-powered wireless cameras that can be recharged via solar power or a hand-crank generator. This way, the cameras won't be dependent on the electrical grid and can continue functioning even during extended power outages.

Wired Systems

While wireless cameras offer flexibility, wired surveillance systems provide higher stability and reliability, particularly in long-term crisis situations. Wired systems are typically harder to disable or tamper with, and they often offer higher-quality video feeds, which can be crucial for identifying intruders or suspicious activity.

If Jack opts for a wired system, he'll need to consider how the wiring will be laid out across the property. He might need to involve a professional to ensure that the system is installed correctly and covers the areas most vulnerable to breach. Wired systems can also be connected to uninterruptible power supplies (UPS) or a backup generator, ensuring continuous operation even during blackouts.

Wired systems are especially beneficial for homes with larger perimeters or when high-definition video is required to monitor wide areas effectively.

Night Vision and Infrared Cameras

Many crisis situations occur under the cover of darkness, so it's crucial for Jack to have night vision or infrared cameras as part of his surveillance system. These cameras allow for clear monitoring even in low-light conditions, giving Jack and his family the ability to detect intruders or animals that might pose a threat.

Night vision cameras use infrared light to illuminate areas that are invisible to the naked eye, ensuring 24/7 coverage of Jack's property. These cameras can be installed near the home's entrance, around the perimeter, and especially near areas like garages or sheds, which are often targeted during break-ins.

If possible, Jack should look for cameras with integrated lighting systems, which can flood an area with light when motion is detected, potentially scaring off intruders before they approach.

Strategic Camera Placement

Once Jack has selected the right equipment, the next step is strategically placing the cameras to ensure maximum coverage of the property. Proper placement is key to creating a comprehensive surveillance system that minimizes blind spots and ensures that every vulnerable entry point is under constant watch.

Covering Entry Points

The first priority should be covering all entry points to the home, including doors, windows, and even basement or garage doors. Jack should place cameras that monitor both the exterior and interior sides of these entry points, ensuring that he can see who is approaching and whether they manage to enter the house.

For instance, a camera positioned above the front door can monitor packages being delivered, people knocking on the door, or potential intruders trying to pick the lock. Similarly, cameras aimed at windows can detect anyone attempting to force their way into the house.

PERIMETER SURVEILLANCE

In addition to securing the home's immediate entry points, Jack should also consider perimeter surveillance. By placing cameras along the property's perimeter, especially at weak spots like gates or areas where fences are low, Jack can detect intruders before they get too close to the house. Motion-detection systems are especially useful for perimeter surveillance, as they can trigger alerts the moment movement is detected.

BLIND SPOT ELIMINATION

Another critical aspect of camera placement is eliminating blind spots. Intruders often look for blind spots in a home's surveillance system, where they can move undetected. Jack should carefully map out his home's layout, identifying areas that might be hidden from direct view—such as behind sheds, in alleyways, or beneath overhangs—and ensure that cameras cover these areas effectively.

Integrating Surveillance with Other Security Systems

For a truly comprehensive security setup, Jack can integrate his surveillance system with other home security measures. For instance, cameras can be synced with motion-sensor lights, alarms, or even smart home systems that notify Jack when unusual activity is detected. Many modern surveillance systems allow for direct integration with smartphone apps, providing Jack with real-time notifications of any breaches, even when he's away from the property.

Additionally, some advanced systems offer two-way audio, allowing Jack to communicate directly with anyone near the cameras. This can be useful for deterring intruders by letting them know they are being watched, or for communicating with family members or visitors outside the home.

Ensuring Surveillance Operates During Crises

One of Jack's main concerns will be ensuring that the surveillance system remains functional during power outages or infrastructure breakdowns. To achieve this, Jack can implement several off-grid solutions, including:

- Solar panels to power cameras and the overall system.
- Battery backups or hand-crank generators to recharge devices.
- Portable power banks specifically dedicated to keeping security systems operational.

By setting up a home surveillance system that operates independently of the main power grid, Jack ensures his family's security even during the most extreme crises.

Staying Informed During a Crisis

In the midst of a crisis, staying informed can be the difference between safety and vulnerability. For Jack and his family, having reliable sources of information helps them make informed decisions, adapt to rapidly changing situations, and stay one step ahead of potential threats. Whether it's a natural disaster, civil unrest, or a long-term power outage, having access to real-time updates about what's happening outside their home is critical for survival.

During a crisis, conventional communication channels like the internet, television, and mobile networks may become unreliable or completely inaccessible. Therefore, it is essential for Jack to have a strategy in place that enables him to receive vital information, even when modern infrastructure fails. This chapter will walk through various methods for staying informed during a crisis, focusing on off-grid solutions that ensure the family remains connected to the outside world no matter the circumstances.

The Role of Information in Crisis Situations

Before diving into specific strategies, it's important to understand why staying informed is so essential during a crisis. Information serves several purposes:

- **Decision-making:** Knowing what's happening around you enables better decisions. Jack and his family may need to decide whether to stay inside, evacuate, or fortify their home based on real-time developments.
- **Anticipating threats:** Understanding the situation outside their immediate area—whether it's looters, weather changes, or other dangers—gives the family the chance to anticipate risks and prepare accordingly.
- **Connecting with authorities:** Updates from local authorities, government agencies, and emergency responders can provide crucial instructions or warnings.
- **Moral support:** In prolonged crises, being aware of what others are going through or how relief efforts are progressing can help keep spirits high.

Using Radios for Reliable Information

One of the most dependable ways to stay informed during a crisis, particularly when other communication networks fail, is through radios. Unlike mobile phones and internet-based platforms that rely on complex infrastructures, radios can function independently, making them a crucial tool for Jack's emergency preparedness plan.

EMERGENCY WEATHER RADIOS

An emergency weather radio is a must-have in any crisis preparedness kit. These radios are designed to provide real-time updates from government agencies like the National Oceanic and Atmospheric Administration (NOAA). Jack can tune in to get accurate, up-to-date weather information, which is particularly important in scenarios like hurricanes, floods, or wildfires, where knowing what's coming next is crucial for safety.

Many emergency radios come equipped with hand-crank or solar-powered charging options, which means Jack won't need to worry about the battery dying when the power grid is down. Some models even include built-in flashlights and USB ports to charge small devices.

SHORTWAVE RADIOS

While emergency weather radios offer regional updates, shortwave radios provide access to international frequencies, which can be invaluable in long-term crises. Shortwave radios can pick up transmissions from broadcasters around the world, allowing Jack to stay informed about the global situation and receive updates even when local communication networks are down.

Shortwave radios can also be used to communicate with others over long distances, making them a versatile tool in crisis situations. For Jack, the ability to send and receive information through shortwave radio ensures that he can stay connected to the outside world, even in a complete communication blackout.

Monitoring Local News and Government Updates

In most crises, local authorities play a pivotal role in providing guidance and support to residents. It's essential that Jack has a way to stay updated on local government announcements, emergency alerts, and important safety information. Even if Jack's internet or mobile networks go down, many cities and counties have contingency plans in place to broadcast emergency updates through radio, loudspeakers, or public address systems.

PORTABLE FM/AM RADIOS

In addition to shortwave and emergency weather radios, portable FM/AM radios are a simple and effective way to tune into local news stations during a crisis. While Jack's family might usually rely on smartphones for news updates, an old-school FM/AM radio can be a lifeline for real-time local information, particularly during power outages or cell network disruptions. It's advisable to keep a battery-powered radio on hand and have spare batteries available in case of prolonged power outages.

COMMUNITY BROADCASTS

Many local governments and community organizations use community broadcast stations to reach residents in times of crisis. Jack should familiarize himself with the local radio stations that broadcast emergency information in his area. These stations may provide critical updates about evacuation routes, shelter locations, and safety measures, particularly during natural disasters like hurricanes or wildfires.

Staying Connected Through HAM Radio

When mainstream communication channels fail, HAM radio is a powerful tool for staying informed and connecting with others in the preparedness community. HAM radios, also known as amateur radios, allow users to communicate over long distances without relying on commercial networks. This makes them ideal for two-way communication during a disaster.

GETTING A HAM RADIO LICENSE

For Jack, investing in a HAM radio could be a game-changer. However, using HAM radios requires a license in most areas. Before the crisis hits, Jack should consider getting his amateur radio license, which allows him to legally operate on HAM frequencies. Licensed operators can communicate with one another across vast distances, providing Jack with an additional layer of security and connection, especially in the event of a complete communication breakdown.

Once Jack is licensed, he can tap into preparedness communities that use HAM radios for disaster communication. These networks often share valuable updates, relay information between regions, and even help coordinate local relief efforts.

Off-Grid Solutions for Digital Communication

Although traditional communication tools like radios are invaluable during a crisis, Jack might still want to rely on digital communication tools as long as they remain operational. To extend the life of his mobile devices and continue using them for as long as possible, Jack can implement off-grid power solutions.

SOLAR-POWERED CHARGERS AND BATTERY BANKS

One of the simplest ways to keep smartphones, tablets, and other digital communication devices running during a power outage is through solar-powered chargers or portable battery banks. Jack should ensure that his home emergency kit includes at least one high-capacity battery bank, which can charge essential devices multiple times before running out of power.

In addition, a solar-powered charger can be used to recharge the battery bank itself or power devices directly, making it a reliable solution for long-term power outages. By keeping his mobile devices charged, Jack will have access to emergency apps, stored maps, and communication tools for as long as the cell networks remain operational.

MESH NETWORKS

Another way to maintain communication in the absence of a traditional network is through mesh networks. Mesh networks allow devices like smartphones and tablets to communicate with each other directly, bypassing centralized cell towers. This decentralized approach makes it possible for Jack to stay in touch with his family, neighbors, and local support groups even when the usual communication infrastructure is down.

While mesh networks require some setup and technical knowledge, they can be highly effective in maintaining local communication during extended crises.

Emergency Alert Apps

Finally, before a crisis hits, Jack can download emergency alert apps that provide real-time updates on local emergencies. These apps often work even when phone service is limited or intermittent, giving Jack crucial information about local weather patterns, evacuation orders, and other emergency protocols.

Some key apps Jack might consider include:

- **FEMA App:** Provides weather alerts and information about disaster relief services.
- **American Red Cross Emergency App:** Offers real-time alerts and instructions on what to do in various emergency situations.
- **Zello Walkie Talkie App:** Turns a smartphone into a walkie-talkie, allowing for instant voice communication with other users.

With the right combination of radio systems, HAM communication, and off-grid power solutions, Jack and his family will be well-prepared to stay informed and connected during any crisis, regardless of the challenges that arise.

Networking with Neighbors and Local Support Groups

In times of crisis, your immediate surroundings and the people within them can make a significant difference in how effectively you manage the situation. When you think about crisis preparedness, it's easy to focus on stockpiling supplies or building strong fortifications for your home, but the human element—your neighbors and local support groups—can be just as critical. Jack, like many preppers, understands that forming a strong network with neighbors and nearby communities isn't just about socializing. It's a fundamental layer of defense and support that will prove invaluable when things go south.

While we often think of preparedness in terms of individual efforts, the reality is that no person, or even family, can survive in isolation for long during an extended crisis. By creating a network of trusted individuals who can share resources, offer skills, and provide emotional support, Jack can amplify his ability to protect his family and ensure their long-term survival. Let's explore how Jack can begin building these networks and why they are essential for resilience.

The Importance of Building Trust in Your Neighborhood

In a crisis scenario, neighbors often become your closest allies. Trust is the foundation of any successful network, and building that trust starts well before any disaster strikes. Jack should get to know his neighbors, particularly those who live near him and could be useful allies in an emergency. For example, if there's a doctor, a skilled carpenter, or someone with security or law enforcement experience living close by, those individuals will bring essential skills to the group. It's critical that Jack approaches these relationships with an open and cooperative mindset, focusing on the idea that mutual survival benefits everyone involved.

In many neighborhoods, particularly suburban or rural areas, a neighborhood watch or local preparedness group might already exist. If Jack's neighborhood doesn't have one, he can take the initiative to form one. This can start as something informal—monthly barbecues or meetings where the topic of preparedness is slowly introduced. Over time, Jack can gauge who is genuinely interested and begin forming a more structured group.

By being proactive and forming relationships early, Jack will have built-in alliances by the time a crisis hits. When things go wrong, the last thing he'll want to do is waste time evaluating who can be trusted or who has resources to contribute. Instead, by fostering these relationships beforehand, he will already know who in his network is reliable, and his neighbors will view him as a credible source of guidance and leadership.

Skills and Resource Sharing Among Neighbors

One of the greatest benefits of networking with neighbors and local support groups is skill-sharing. Each household in Jack's community is likely to have different strengths, whether that's knowledge of first aid, food preservation, carpentry, or even child care. A well-rounded network will complement Jack's skills and offer valuable services that he alone may not be equipped to provide.

For example, while Jack may be well-versed in setting up off-grid energy solutions, he might lack experience in gardening or food production. A neighbor with a green thumb could help sustain the group's food supply, while Jack could provide technical assistance in exchange. This mutual exchange of knowledge and skills not only makes the group more resilient but also builds camaraderie and trust.

Additionally, resource sharing can provide Jack and his family with more flexibility in managing limited supplies. In an extended crisis, no one will have everything they need.

However, if Jack's neighbors are open to sharing resources such as extra water filtration systems, medical supplies, or solar power generators, everyone benefits. To facilitate this, Jack could work with his neighbors to create a resource inventory that tracks who has access to certain essential items. This helps ensure that no household is left without critical supplies and allows the group to avoid redundancies.

Forming Local Support Groups

Beyond neighbors, Jack should also consider forming or joining local support groups specifically designed to prepare for disasters. These groups could operate on a larger scale than just his neighborhood, incorporating individuals from nearby areas who may bring additional skills, resources, and perspectives.

Local support groups often meet regularly to discuss various aspects of preparedness— whether it's reviewing evacuation plans, learning first aid, or practicing defensive drills. These groups may also offer Jack access to a broader range of resources, including bulk-buying opportunities for long-term food storage or emergency medical supplies. The strength of these groups lies in their ability to pool resources and knowledge, providing Jack with a deeper network of people who can support him when disaster strikes.

Some cities and towns also have community emergency response teams (CERTs) that work in conjunction with local government. Jack should look into whether his area offers CERT training, as this provides specialized skills in areas like search and rescue, disaster medical operations, and fire suppression.

Creating a Communication Plan with Neighbors

Once Jack has formed connections with his neighbors and local support groups, the next step is to establish a communication plan. In a disaster, traditional communication networks like cell towers and the internet may go down, so Jack needs to ensure that his group has alternative ways to stay connected.

A simple but effective method is setting up walkie-talkies or two-way radios for quick and direct communication between nearby households. Jack should work with his group to assign specific channels for emergency use, and practice regular communication drills to ensure everyone knows what to do if lines of communication go down.

Collaborating on Security and Defense

One of the primary reasons for forming a network with neighbors is security. In a long-term crisis, defending against potential threats, such as looters or other desperate individuals, becomes a critical concern. While Jack may have prepared his home with strong fortifications and surveillance, those measures are amplified when they're part of a neighborhood-wide defense plan.

Jack and his neighbors can develop a plan to coordinate security patrols, share surveillance footage, and establish early-warning systems. By pooling resources like motion detectors, night-vision cameras, or even guard dogs, the entire community will be better protected. Moreover, by working together, the neighborhood will present a more formidable presence to outsiders who might otherwise target isolated homes.

Emotional and Moral Support

Finally, it's important not to underestimate the value of emotional and moral support that comes from networking with others. In an extended crisis, isolation can lead to mental health challenges, including anxiety, depression, and panic. Jack's family will benefit greatly from maintaining human connections during tough times. Regular contact with others—whether it's checking in on neighbors, hosting group dinners, or sharing stories of survival—provides a sense of normalcy and comfort.

Neighbors can also help each other deal with psychological first aid, providing guidance and care when individuals in the community experience high levels of stress or trauma. This emotional connection fosters resilience, making the community stronger and more cohesive in the face of adversity.

Networking with neighbors and local support groups is about more than just sharing supplies and skills—it's about creating a unified front that increases the likelihood of survival for everyone involved. For Jack and his family, these connections will be their lifeline during a crisis, providing them with the strength and resources they need to weather any storm.

CHAPTER 8

PERSONALIZED EMERGENCY PLANS FOR YOUR FAMILY

Creating a Crisis Response Plan for Your Family

When it comes to preparing for any type of emergency or disaster, one of the most crucial steps you can take is to create a clear and actionable crisis response plan for your family. This plan serves as a roadmap for how each member of the household should act in the event of a crisis, ensuring that everyone knows their role, where to go, what to bring, and how to communicate. Jack, like many responsible individuals preparing for unpredictable times, understands that having a well-structured family crisis response plan could mean the difference between life and death.

A solid crisis response plan not only alleviates the stress and confusion that arises during chaotic situations but also instills confidence and a sense of preparedness in every family member. Here's how Jack can go about creating a personalized plan that's designed to address the unique needs and dynamics of his household.

Step 1: Assessing Your Family's Specific Needs and Risks

Every family is different, and no single crisis response plan will suit all households. Jack's first step in creating an effective plan is to evaluate his family's specific needs. This includes identifying vulnerabilities, such as health concerns, young children, elderly family members, or pets. Each of these factors will influence the way the plan is structured.

- **Medical needs:** If a family member has a chronic condition or requires daily medication, Jack should ensure that the plan accounts for this. He'll need to have a stockpile of essential medicines, clearly labeled, and accessible in an emergency. Moreover, he should create a schedule for rotating these medicines to prevent expiration.

- **Family dynamics:** If Jack's family includes young children, he'll need to simplify and explain the plan in a way that they can understand and follow. Regular drills will ensure that even the youngest members of the family know what to do.

- **Geographic risks:** Another factor to consider is geographic location. If Jack's home is in an area prone to natural disasters, such as hurricanes, earthquakes, or floods, the plan should address specific actions for those events. For example, a family living in a wildfire-prone area may need to plan for quick evacuation, while a family in a flood zone might prepare to seek higher ground or stay in a fortified location.

Step 2: Establishing Clear Roles and Responsibilities

Once Jack has identified the specific needs of his family, the next step is to establish clear roles and responsibilities for each person in the household. Assigning tasks ahead of time reduces confusion during an emergency, allowing everyone to act quickly and efficiently. This is particularly important in families with multiple members, as having each person know their role helps ensure that critical tasks aren't overlooked.

For instance:

- **Jack:** As the head of the household, Jack may take on the role of gathering critical supplies (water, food, first aid) and securing the home. This could involve fortifying windows, locking down entry points, or turning off utilities like gas and electricity to prevent further hazards.
- **His spouse:** Jack's spouse could be responsible for gathering important documents and ensuring that the family's emergency contact list is up-to-date. This might include passports, birth certificates, and insurance documents, which should be stored in a waterproof, easily accessible location.
- **Older children:** If Jack has teenage children, they can assist by helping younger siblings or taking charge of preparing the family's "go bags" (pre-packed emergency kits with essentials like food, water, clothing, and flashlights).

It's essential to review these roles regularly and update them as family dynamics change. Regular rehearsals of the plan, especially when new skills or tools are introduced, help ensure everyone remains comfortable and confident in their role.

Step 3: Setting Up Evacuation Routes and Meeting Points

An effective family crisis plan should always include clear evacuation routes and designated meeting points. Jack needs to think through scenarios where his family would need to leave the home quickly, either due to an immediate threat like a house fire or a more widespread disaster, such as a hurricane or civil unrest.

- **Primary and secondary routes:** Jack should establish both primary and secondary evacuation routes from the home. For instance, the primary route could be through the front door and into a car parked in the driveway, while the secondary route might involve using a window to access a backyard and hopping a fence if the front exit is blocked. These routes should be rehearsed so that everyone knows how to exit safely under pressure.
- **Local and distant meeting points:** The family also needs designated meeting points in case they become separated. Jack should choose two: one close to home (perhaps a nearby park or school) and one farther away (a friend's house or public shelter). The

local meeting point is useful for situations where the family can quickly reconvene, while the distant location provides a fallback if the entire neighborhood or region is unsafe.

Step 4: Communication Plans and Backup Options

In the chaos of an emergency, communication can often break down. That's why it's important for Jack to create a communication plan that includes both primary and backup methods for staying in touch with family members, neighbors, and local authorities.

- **Cell phones:** While cell phones may be the most obvious form of communication, Jack should have backup options in case the power grid or cell towers go down. It's a good idea to invest in two-way radios or walkie-talkies that work over short distances. These can be distributed among family members, allowing them to stay in touch even if cellular networks are overloaded or offline.
- **Emergency contact list:** Jack should compile a list of emergency contacts that includes not only close relatives and friends but also local law enforcement, medical professionals, and community shelters. This list should be easily accessible and shared with every family member.
- **Out-of-area contact:** It's wise for Jack's family to have an out-of-area contact person—someone located far enough away that they would be unaffected by a localized disaster. This person can act as a communication hub if family members become separated or unable to reach each other. Each member of the family should know how to contact this individual, and Jack can instruct them to check in with this person at regular intervals during a crisis.

Step 5: Packing and Storing Emergency Kits

Another essential component of Jack's crisis response plan is to ensure that each family member has an emergency kit packed and ready to go. These kits, often referred to as "go bags," should include enough supplies to sustain each person for 72 hours. The goal is to have everything needed for short-term survival in a crisis, while also having additional supplies stored at home for longer-term needs.

- **Essentials:** Go bags should include water, non-perishable food, clothing, blankets, a first aid kit, and tools such as multi-purpose knives or flashlights. Each bag should be tailored to the individual's specific needs. For example, Jack's children might need comfort items, while his spouse's bag could include extra medications or important documents.
- **Regular rotation:** Items like food, water, and medicine have expiration dates, so Jack should develop a system for regularly rotating these items. Every few months, the family should review their go bags, update any outdated supplies, and ensure that everything is in good working order.

Step 6: Regular Practice and Drills

Having a well-written plan is only effective if every family member knows how to execute it. Jack's family should practice their emergency plan through regular drills. These drills should simulate different scenarios, such as evacuating due to a fire, locking down the house during a storm, or communicating during a grid failure.

Practicing these scenarios will reduce panic during a real crisis and help the family react calmly and effectively. The more familiar they are with their roles and responsibilities, the more confident they'll be when the unexpected occurs.

Monthly Preparedness Checklists

Creating a crisis response plan is only part of the equation when it comes to ensuring your family is ready for any unexpected event. Maintaining a state of readiness is crucial, and this requires consistent attention to the various elements of preparedness. A well-designed monthly preparedness checklist helps ensure that every aspect of your emergency plan is up-to-date, functional, and able to be implemented immediately when needed.

For Jack, his family, and countless others in the preparedness community, a monthly checklist is a practical tool that breaks down overwhelming tasks into manageable steps, allowing each family member to contribute while minimizing the anxiety that can accompany crisis preparation. Let's explore how a tailored monthly checklist can keep Jack's family organized, confident, and ready for anything.

Step 1: Stockpile Review and Rotation

One of the most essential components of any family's emergency plan is their stockpile of food, water, and medical supplies. Ensuring that these items are not only available but also fresh and viable when a crisis hits is critical. Jack's monthly checklist should include a dedicated section for reviewing and rotating stockpiled items.

- **Food and water:** Jack should regularly inspect his family's stored food and water to check for expiration dates, spoilage, or damage. Canned goods, dry goods, and freeze-dried meals need to be rotated out and replaced with fresh supplies. It's important to establish a rotation schedule to avoid wastage. Likewise, water should be stored in sanitized containers and replenished periodically to ensure freshness and safety.

- **Medical supplies:** Similarly, Jack should review the family's medical supplies, including over-the-counter medications, first aid items, and prescription medicines. Bandages, ointments, and antiseptics can expire or lose their effectiveness over time, so it's crucial to check expiration dates and replace anything that is nearing the end of its shelf life.

- **Fuel:** If Jack relies on fuel sources like propane, gasoline, or kerosene for backup power or cooking, he should check and replenish his reserves monthly. Fuel degrades over time, so adding stabilizers or rotating stored fuel will ensure it remains useful during an emergency.

Step 2: Equipment Check and Maintenance

Another critical part of Jack's monthly checklist is assessing the condition and functionality of the family's emergency equipment. From flashlights to generators, everything should be in proper working order before it's needed.

- **Power and light sources:** Jack should regularly test the family's flashlights, lanterns, and portable power banks to ensure they work properly. He should also check the batteries and keep spares readily available. Solar-powered or hand-crank options are excellent backups that should also be reviewed monthly.
- **Generators:** If Jack's family has a generator, it needs regular maintenance to ensure it starts when needed. This could include testing the generator for operational functionality, checking fuel levels, and inspecting it for any signs of wear or damage.
- **Communications:** In the event of a grid-down situation, Jack's family may need to rely on two-way radios or HAM radios to stay in touch. These devices should be tested monthly, and backup batteries or alternative power sources should be kept on hand. Jack could also include monthly communication drills to practice using these radios effectively in case of an emergency.
- **First aid kits and fire extinguishers:** Medical supplies and fire safety equipment also require monthly inspection. Jack should check the expiration dates on first aid supplies and ensure fire extinguishers are fully charged and in good working order. This is an often overlooked but essential part of a preparedness plan.

Step 3: Reviewing the Family's Go Bags

Go bags (also known as bug-out bags) are one of the most critical items in any emergency plan, and Jack should dedicate part of his monthly checklist to reviewing and updating each family member's go bag. These bags need to be packed with essential items that can sustain the family for at least 72 hours if they have to evacuate quickly.

- **Personalized contents:** Each go bag should be tailored to the specific needs of the individual. For example, Jack's children may need extra clothing or comfort items, while his spouse's go bag might require additional medication or documents.
- **Refreshing consumables:** Water, snacks, and other consumables in the go bags should be checked and rotated regularly to ensure nothing is expired. Clothing should be swapped out for seasonally appropriate options, ensuring that every family member has what they need, regardless of the weather.
- **Tools and gear:** It's important to check that any tools, such as multi-tools, knives, or fire starters, are in good working condition. Jack should also ensure that items like emergency blankets, flashlights, and ponchos are still intact and functional.

Step 4: Updating Emergency Contacts and Plans

Another essential task on the monthly checklist is reviewing and updating the family's emergency contacts and crisis response plan. Over time, people's lives and circumstances change, so it's important to keep this information current.

- **Emergency contact list:** Jack should review and update the family's list of emergency contacts, ensuring that phone numbers, addresses, and other important details are still accurate. This list should include family members, neighbors, friends, and any local emergency services or shelters that could be contacted in a crisis.
- **Out-of-area contact:** It's also a good idea to ensure that an out-of-area contact is still accessible and willing to serve as a communication hub in case of separation during an emergency. Jack's family should review how to reach this person using backup communication methods.
- **Evacuation routes and meeting points:** Jack should revisit the family's pre-determined evacuation routes and meeting points. Any changes in local infrastructure, weather patterns, or neighborhood dynamics could require adjustments to these plans. Jack's family should practice their evacuation routes and update any maps or instructions that are included in their go bags.

Step 5: Skills and Training

Preparedness isn't just about having the right supplies; it's also about having the skills to survive. Each month, Jack should incorporate a review of the family's skill set, focusing on areas where they can improve or refresh their knowledge.

- **First aid and medical training:** The family should review basic first aid skills, ensuring that everyone knows how to perform CPR, treat wounds, and manage other common injuries. Jack might also consider scheduling first aid courses or watching instructional videos as a family.
- **Fire safety drills:** Practicing fire safety is another essential part of preparedness. Jack's monthly checklist should include a review of fire escape routes, the proper use of fire extinguishers, and strategies for handling smoke or flame-related emergencies.
- **Communication drills:** Jack's family should regularly practice using their backup communication devices, such as walkie-talkies or HAM radios, to ensure they can communicate effectively in a crisis. This practice will help eliminate confusion and ensure that everyone is comfortable with the equipment.

Step 6: Practicing and Adjusting the Plan

The final part of Jack's monthly preparedness checklist involves putting everything into practice. Simply having a plan on paper won't be enough if the family isn't comfortable executing it. Jack should schedule regular practice drills to review evacuation routes, go bag contents, and other aspects of the family's crisis plan.

- **Family drills:** Monthly drills help familiarize the family with different scenarios, reducing panic and confusion during a real crisis. Jack could simulate situations such as a power outage, a severe storm, or a fire to help the family practice their roles and responsibilities.
- **Adjusting for feedback:** After each drill, Jack should gather feedback from his family members to see what worked and what didn't. These insights can help him adjust and improve the plan, making it more efficient and tailored to his family's evolving needs.

By keeping a detailed monthly preparedness checklist, Jack ensures that his family remains ready for whatever comes their way. Regular reviews and drills instill confidence and build resilience, providing peace of mind that they can face any challenge with preparedness and strength.

Adapting Plans to Geographic Risks

When crafting an emergency plan for your family, one of the most crucial aspects is adapting that plan to account for the unique geographic risks of your region. Geographic location significantly influences the type of disasters or crises you may face, from hurricanes in coastal regions to wildfires in arid zones. Each area has its specific vulnerabilities, and preparing for these localized threats can make the difference between an effective response and one that leaves your family in jeopardy.

For Jack, understanding his family's geographic risks means taking a thorough look at the region where they live, analyzing historical data, and crafting a plan tailored to the specific challenges that come with their location. Let's dive deeper into how geographic risks can shape preparedness and what steps Jack can take to ensure his family is ready for the unexpected.

Identifying Geographic Risks

The first step in adapting an emergency plan is identifying the specific geographic risks that affect your area. This requires understanding the common natural disasters, environmental hazards, and potential infrastructural issues that may arise. Different regions face a wide variety of threats, so it's important to research thoroughly.

- **Natural disasters:** Jack should begin by identifying the most common natural disasters in his area. For example, if he lives in Florida, hurricanes may be his primary concern. In California, the risk of wildfires or earthquakes may take precedence. Tornadoes, floods, and winter storms are also region-specific risks that need to be addressed in any emergency plan. Knowing the primary threats helps Jack focus his preparations on the most likely scenarios.
- **Man-made risks:** Geographic risks aren't limited to natural disasters. Urban areas may face threats like power outages, industrial accidents, or civil unrest, while rural regions

might be more susceptible to infrastructure failures. Jack must account for potential man-made risks, ensuring that his family's plan covers situations that could disrupt everyday life in his particular environment.

- **Climate considerations:** Geography also affects the climate, which in turn impacts preparedness. For instance, desert regions may require plans that prioritize water storage and heat mitigation, while northern areas may focus on staying warm during prolonged winter power outages. Jack should consider the year-round weather patterns in his region and adapt his family's plan accordingly.

Customizing Emergency Supplies for Geographic Risks

Once Jack has identified the geographic risks, it's time to ensure that his family's emergency supplies reflect these threats. Stockpiling generic supplies like food and water is essential, but region-specific items are also crucial to ensure his family's survival in a localized disaster.

- **Water and flood barriers:** In flood-prone areas, Jack should invest in sandbags or other flood barriers to protect his home. Additionally, waterproof storage containers are essential for keeping important documents and electronics safe. He might also consider purchasing a sump pump or having one installed in the basement to prevent flooding during heavy rains.
- **Fireproof materials:** If Jack's home is located in a wildfire-prone region, he should stock up on fire-retardant materials to safeguard his property. A comprehensive wildfire evacuation kit should include masks for smoke inhalation, fire blankets, and high-powered water hoses. It's also important to maintain defensible space around the property, clearing any flammable vegetation.
- **Cold-weather gear:** In areas with harsh winters, Jack should ensure his family has access to cold-weather gear and supplies. This includes thermal blankets, backup heating methods, and plenty of winter clothing. Additionally, non-perishable food items that don't require cooking in case of power outages are crucial for surviving winter storms.

By tailoring emergency supplies to the specific geographic risks, Jack ensures that his family has the tools and resources to face their region's challenges head-on.

Planning Evacuation Routes Based on Geographic Terrain

Evacuations are a key part of many emergency plans, and Jack must consider how his location affects his family's ability to evacuate quickly and safely. This is where geography plays a significant role, as the local terrain can either aid or hinder evacuation efforts.

- **Escape routes:** If Jack lives in an area prone to hurricanes or wildfires, evacuation routes are essential. He should have multiple planned routes in case primary roads are blocked or inaccessible. In some cases, local authorities may provide specific evacuation routes, but it's critical that Jack and his family have alternate paths mapped out, especially in areas with limited road access.

- **Traffic congestion:** For families in urban areas, evacuation can be challenging due to heavy traffic during emergencies. Jack should monitor local traffic patterns and identify alternative backroads or less congested routes. Pre-arranged meeting points outside of the city can help reduce confusion and ensure the family stays together during a chaotic evacuation.

- **Rural challenges:** Conversely, rural residents may face difficulties due to limited infrastructure or lack of nearby evacuation routes. Jack should ensure that his family has adequate fuel reserves for long distances and plans that account for longer evacuation times. He may also need to plan for sheltering in place for extended periods if evacuation is not a viable option due to geographic isolation.

Developing Response Strategies for Specific Local Threats

In addition to evacuation planning, Jack needs to develop response strategies that are directly influenced by his geographic location. Each type of disaster requires a different response, and understanding these specific threats will enable Jack to create a comprehensive and effective plan.

- **Hurricane preparedness:** If Jack lives in a hurricane zone, his plan should focus on securing his home, ensuring adequate supplies of water, food, and medical provisions, and preparing for potential long-term power outages. This may include installing hurricane shutters or reinforcing doors and windows.

- **Earthquake response:** In earthquake-prone areas, Jack should practice "Drop, Cover, and Hold On" drills with his family. Additionally, securing heavy furniture, appliances, and breakable items will reduce the risk of injury during a quake. Having an emergency radio to receive alerts about aftershocks or further risks is also crucial.

- **Wildfire protection:** Wildfire preparedness involves creating an evacuation plan that accounts for rapidly changing fire paths. Jack should ensure his family knows how to shut off gas and electricity in case the home is compromised. A portable generator may be necessary in case power lines are affected by the fire.

By developing localized response strategies, Jack ensures that his family is prepared to react swiftly and appropriately to the unique geographic risks they face.

Practicing Drills that Reflect Geographic Realities

Emergency drills are a powerful tool for solidifying an emergency plan and giving Jack's family the confidence they need to respond in a crisis. However, these drills must reflect the specific geographic risks that the family is likely to encounter.

- **Seasonal drills:** Since many geographic risks follow seasonal patterns, it's important to schedule drills throughout the year that reflect these realities. For example, hurricane drills may be best practiced during the summer and fall, while winter storm preparedness can be the focus in late fall and early winter. This helps keep the family's skills sharp and relevant.

- **Simulating local threats:** Jack should also design drills that simulate the specific threats his region is prone to, whether it's practicing wildfire evacuations or running through flood preparedness steps. Regular drills help the family remain familiar with their roles and responsibilities, reducing the chance of panic when an actual emergency occurs.

By focusing on the unique risks that geographic location presents, Jack ensures his family's emergency plan is not just a one-size-fits-all solution but a tailored and strategic plan of action. Localized preparedness is a crucial step toward building a resilient and adaptable family capable of surviving whatever comes their way.

Training Drills for the Whole Family

Preparing for a crisis is not just about stockpiling supplies or creating a response plan; it's also about ensuring that every family member knows what to do in high-pressure situations. A well-crafted plan is only effective if everyone can execute it without hesitation, and this is where training drills come in. For Jack and his family, regular drills tailored to specific emergencies are essential for building the confidence and skills needed to respond efficiently when disaster strikes. It's a proactive way to eliminate uncertainty and foster a sense of calm during chaotic situations.

Why Family Drills Matter

Training drills help condition both adults and children to respond swiftly and correctly during emergencies. By repeatedly practicing, the body and mind learn to act instinctively, reducing panic and confusion. For Jack's family, this can be the difference between a coordinated escape from a wildfire or a delayed response that puts lives at risk. These drills allow everyone to practice their roles and familiarize themselves with the tools and equipment needed during a crisis. More importantly, they offer Jack's family the opportunity to spot weaknesses in their emergency plan and refine their strategy before it's too late.

- **Reducing fear and anxiety:** For children and adults alike, the uncertainty of an emergency situation can induce anxiety. Regular drills help demystify these situations, offering reassurance that there's a clear, actionable plan in place. This reduces fear, and family members are less likely to freeze or make mistakes during an actual crisis.
- **Building muscle memory:** Drills create muscle memory. When faced with stress, our brains often revert to what's been practiced most. By running through a fire evacuation drill, for instance, Jack's family will automatically remember where to go, how to exit the house safely, and where to meet outside. This ingrained knowledge could save precious time when every second counts.
- **Identifying potential pitfalls:** During practice, Jack may realize that certain exits are less accessible than they thought, or that younger children may struggle with carrying

essential supplies. Drills allow for these weaknesses to be addressed, offering a chance to adjust the plan or provide additional training.

Types of Drills to Practice

The types of drills Jack's family should practice depend on the risks their region is most vulnerable to. However, a comprehensive family training routine should include multiple scenarios to ensure preparedness across various emergencies. Each drill should focus on executing the family's crisis plan effectively, with everyone performing their assigned roles.

- **Fire drills:** Every family should practice fire evacuation drills regularly, given how quickly house fires can spread. Jack's family needs to know the fastest ways to exit the house from every room, where to gather outside, and how to help younger or elderly family members who may need assistance. Fire drills should also include practicing how to handle smoke inhalation, using fire extinguishers, and testing fire alarms.
- **Earthquake drills:** For those living in earthquake-prone regions, like California, practicing earthquake safety is critical. Jack's family should practice "Drop, Cover, and Hold On" procedures, ensuring everyone knows to get under a sturdy table or desk during shaking. They should also identify safe spots in every room where family members can take cover away from windows and heavy furniture that may topple over.
- **Flood and evacuation drills:** In flood-prone areas, evacuation may be necessary. Jack should ensure that his family has practiced how to quickly gather their emergency kits and leave the house safely. They need to know their designated evacuation routes, as well as how to shut off utilities like gas and electricity before leaving. If roads are flooded, the family must also have alternative routes mapped out and practice traveling to higher ground.

Conducting Drills for Different Family Members

Jack's family includes people of various ages, physical abilities, and levels of understanding. To ensure that everyone is equally prepared, drills should be tailored to meet the needs of each individual while still maintaining the overall structure of the family plan.

- **Drills for young children:** Children, especially those under 10, may find emergency drills overwhelming. To ensure that they participate fully without becoming frightened, it's important to make drills engaging and easy to understand. Jack might consider turning drills into a game by rewarding participation with praise or small incentives. He can also simplify instructions, focusing on key points like "stay low and crawl out if there's smoke" or "go to our meeting spot as quickly as possible."
- **Drills for older adults or family members with special needs:** Some family members may require extra assistance during an emergency. Jack should ensure that drills account for any mobility issues or medical conditions. For instance, they may need to assign a family member to assist an elderly relative or prepare medical supplies in case of an evacuation. Practicing these specific roles ensures everyone knows how to help vulnerable members during a crisis.

- **Role assignments for teenagers and adults:** Teenagers and adults can take on more responsibility during a crisis, such as checking on younger siblings, gathering essential supplies, or communicating with emergency responders. During drills, Jack should delegate specific tasks to each family member, such as assigning one person to grab the first aid kit while another checks that all windows and doors are locked. Practicing these roles ensures that everyone knows exactly what they're responsible for when the time comes.

Keeping Drills Engaging and Regular

One of the biggest challenges with family drills is ensuring they don't become monotonous. Jack can avoid this by keeping the drills engaging and using different methods to challenge his family. For example, practicing a fire drill in the middle of the night simulates a more realistic scenario and tests how well everyone reacts when they're groggy or disoriented. Similarly, running an evacuation drill when the family is out at a park or at a friend's house offers valuable practice in responding when they're away from home.

- **Randomizing drills:** The unpredictability of a real emergency is part of what makes it so stressful. To prepare for this, Jack can randomly schedule drills throughout the year, so his family never knows when one will happen. This keeps everyone on their toes and ensures that they are ready to act at any moment.
- **Incorporating surprise elements:** Jack might add challenges to drills to make them more realistic. For instance, during an evacuation drill, he can block off one of the regular exits, forcing the family to find an alternative route. This helps prepare them for situations where their usual plan might be compromised.
- **Reviewing and improving:** After each drill, Jack should gather his family to discuss what went well and what could be improved. By reviewing their performance together, they can address any mistakes and make adjustments to their plan. This feedback loop is essential for refining the family's readiness over time.

Reinforcing the Importance of Drills

Finally, it's important that Jack reinforces the purpose behind these drills. His family, particularly younger children, may not fully understand why they're doing this. Jack should explain that these drills are meant to keep everyone safe and prepared for the unexpected. By instilling a sense of responsibility and teamwork, Jack can help his family appreciate the importance of practice and readiness in times of crisis.

Regular training drills, when done thoughtfully and engagingly, provide the peace of mind that Jack's family is prepared for whatever emergency they may face. Through repetition, adaptation, and commitment, they'll develop the skills needed to navigate crises with confidence and efficiency.

Documenting and Storing Emergency Plans

Creating a well-thought-out crisis response plan is only the first step in family preparedness. The next crucial task is ensuring that the plan is properly documented, easily accessible, and securely stored. Having a plan that is clear, concise, and documented helps eliminate confusion during an emergency, particularly when emotions run high and stress levels peak. For Jack and his family, documenting their emergency plans is about ensuring that everyone can refer to the procedures and roles they have practiced, even when the situation becomes overwhelming.

Why Documentation Is Essential

While it's tempting to rely on memory when preparing for emergencies, human recall is often unreliable under stress. By documenting every aspect of the family's emergency plans, Jack can ensure that nothing is left to chance. Documentation provides a reference point for every family member, reinforcing their roles and responsibilities in real-time. This is particularly important for children, elderly family members, or anyone who might forget specific tasks during a crisis.

- **Clarity under pressure:** Emergencies often come with heightened anxiety, and clear documentation can help reduce the risk of panic-induced mistakes. Having everything laid out in a physical document allows family members to quickly review the plan and follow the steps accurately without second-guessing or arguing about what needs to be done.
- **Ensuring consistency:** Documenting the plan ensures that everyone in the family is on the same page. There are no variations or misinterpretations. Jack's family can follow the documented steps without confusion, making sure that everyone's actions are synchronized.
- **Tracking updates and changes:** As Jack's family grows or their geographic location changes, the plan may need to be updated. Documenting the plan makes it easier to track these adjustments. By dating the document and including notes about specific updates, Jack ensures that everyone is aware of any changes to the original plan.

What to Include in the Document

A comprehensive emergency plan document should include all critical information the family needs to act swiftly and efficiently. Jack should approach this process systematically, breaking the document down into key sections for clarity.

- **Roles and responsibilities:** Jack should clearly outline each family member's role during an emergency. This includes who is responsible for gathering supplies, who will manage communications, and who will assist vulnerable family members like young children or elderly relatives. Having these roles clearly defined in the document eliminates any potential confusion when the emergency occurs.

- **Emergency contact information:** The document should include the phone numbers of emergency services, close relatives, neighbors, and local support groups. Additionally, Jack should note the addresses of nearby emergency shelters and hospitals. Including both electronic and paper copies of contact information ensures that it is available even if digital devices fail.

- **Evacuation routes and meeting points:** Jack's family must have documented evacuation routes both inside and outside the home. These routes should account for different types of emergencies, such as fires, floods, or earthquakes. Additionally, Jack should clearly state the designated meeting points for the family, both in and out of the home, and provide instructions for what to do if family members become separated.

- **Supply checklists:** Every emergency plan document should include detailed lists of the supplies needed for each scenario. These lists should be regularly checked, and the document should note the frequency of supply checks to ensure that food, water, and medications remain viable.

- **Medical and special needs considerations:** Jack should include specific instructions for handling medical needs during an emergency, such as how to administer medications or operate medical devices. The plan should also address any additional considerations for family members with disabilities or chronic health conditions.

Storing the Plan Safely

Once Jack has carefully documented the family's emergency plan, the next step is ensuring that the document is stored safely and is readily accessible during an emergency. Storing the plan in multiple formats and locations ensures that Jack's family can access it even if one copy is destroyed or inaccessible.

- **Physical copies:** Every family member should have a printed copy of the emergency plan stored in an easily accessible location. Jack could store these copies in the family's emergency supply kits, as well as in key locations around the house, such as in the kitchen, living room, and bedrooms. Physical copies are essential because they do not rely on electricity or technology, which could fail during a crisis.

- **Digital backups:** In addition to physical copies, Jack should ensure that the emergency plan is stored digitally. This can include saving the document on cloud storage platforms, USB drives, and personal devices like smartphones or tablets. Jack should consider sharing digital copies with trusted relatives or friends who can assist the family in an emergency if necessary.

- **Fireproof and waterproof containers:** To protect the physical copies of the emergency plan from damage, Jack should store them in fireproof and waterproof containers. This ensures that the plan remains intact and usable even if the home is damaged by fire, flood, or other disasters. Small fireproof document safes are ideal for this purpose, and they can be kept in easily accessible areas of the house.

- **On-the-go accessibility:** Emergencies don't always happen when the family is at home. To account for this, Jack should ensure that a portable version of the emergency plan is included in every family member's go-bag. This way, each person can access the plan if they need to evacuate quickly, whether they are at school, work, or elsewhere.

Reviewing and Updating the Plan

An emergency plan is not a static document. Jack should schedule regular family meetings to review the plan and update it as necessary. By involving every family member in the review process, Jack reinforces the importance of preparedness and ensures that everyone remains familiar with the procedures.

- **Annual reviews:** Once a year, Jack's family should conduct a comprehensive review of the emergency plan. During this review, they should assess whether any new risks have emerged, whether any roles need to be reassigned, and whether any supplies have expired. Updating the document during these reviews ensures that the plan remains relevant and functional.
- **Post-drill updates:** After conducting training drills or facing real-life emergency scenarios, Jack should use the feedback from these experiences to improve the plan. If any part of the plan didn't go smoothly during a drill, Jack should make changes to the document, ensuring that the lessons learned are reflected in the updated version.

Reinforcing the Importance of Documentation

Finally, it's essential for Jack to reinforce with his family why documenting the emergency plan is so crucial. Documentation transforms abstract preparation into tangible actions that the family can rely on. It gives them a sense of control and confidence, knowing that they have a roadmap to follow when the unexpected happens. By maintaining this mindset, Jack ensures that his family remains calm, organized, and ready to face any crisis with a clear plan in hand.

A well-documented and securely stored emergency plan is one of the most valuable tools Jack's family can have in their preparedness arsenal. It's not just a piece of paper – it's a lifeline that provides structure and guidance when they need it most.

CHAPTER 9

EMERGING THREATS AND LONG-TERM PREPAREDNESS

- -

Assessing New Global Threats

The modern world is constantly evolving, with new threats emerging at an unprecedented rate. As Jack assesses these dangers, he knows that simply preparing for past crises is not enough. To safeguard his family and home, Jack must stay informed about the latest global threats, analyze how they may impact his specific situation, and adjust his preparedness plan accordingly. In today's world, threats come from a range of sources, including natural disasters, geopolitical conflicts, cyberattacks, pandemics, and climate change. Understanding these risks and their potential consequences is critical to building resilience in an uncertain future.

The Changing Landscape of Global Threats

The scope and scale of global threats have expanded significantly over the past few decades. While natural disasters like hurricanes, floods, and earthquakes remain perennial concerns, new challenges have arisen that require Jack to think beyond traditional disaster preparedness. Emerging threats are often interconnected, creating complex situations that can destabilize communities, governments, and economies.

- **Climate change:** One of the most pressing global threats is climate change, which has far-reaching consequences for natural disasters, resource availability, and geopolitical stability. As global temperatures rise, Jack must consider the increased frequency and intensity of weather-related events such as hurricanes, droughts, and wildfires. Additionally, climate change can disrupt food and water supplies, forcing communities to compete for limited resources, which could lead to social unrest.

- **Geopolitical instability:** In an increasingly interconnected world, regional conflicts can have global repercussions. Political tensions, trade disputes, and resource scarcity can trigger wars or economic sanctions, affecting supply chains and access to essential goods. Jack must stay informed about geopolitical hotspots, particularly those that may disrupt energy supplies or lead to a refugee crisis, which could increase local pressures and security risks.

- **Cyberattacks and infrastructure vulnerability:** As society becomes more reliant on technology, cyberattacks have become a significant threat to national security, business operations, and personal privacy. Critical infrastructure, including power grids, water supplies, and transportation networks, is increasingly vulnerable to cyberattacks. Jack must evaluate how his home and community depend on technology and consider backup plans for when these systems fail.

Evaluating Personal and Regional Risks

For Jack, assessing global threats means narrowing the focus to those that pose the greatest risk to his family's location, lifestyle, and resources. It's essential for him to evaluate how these threats could directly impact his day-to-day life, and which are most likely to require immediate action.

- **Local climate and natural disasters:** Depending on where Jack lives, certain natural disasters may pose a greater risk than others. For example, if Jack resides in a coastal area, hurricanes and flooding may be his primary concern, whereas someone in the Midwest might prioritize tornado preparedness. Understanding the specific vulnerabilities of his region allows Jack to tailor his emergency plan accordingly, including evacuation routes, home fortification measures, and emergency supply stockpiling.
- **Access to critical resources:** Water, energy, and food are vital to surviving any long-term crisis. Jack must consider the availability of these resources in his area, both during normal times and in the event of a disruption. Does his community rely on a single power plant or water source? Are there alternative routes for food supplies in case of shortages? By evaluating these factors, Jack can identify weak points in his local infrastructure and plan for contingencies.
- **Health and pandemics:** The COVID-19 pandemic demonstrated how a global health crisis could rapidly escalate, straining healthcare systems and disrupting daily life. For Jack, this experience underscores the importance of monitoring global health trends and understanding the potential impact of new diseases. Preparedness includes stockpiling medical supplies, staying informed about vaccination developments, and having a plan for quarantine or isolation if necessary.

The Role of Media and Information in Threat Assessment

One of the most significant challenges in assessing global threats is distinguishing between accurate information and misinformation. With the proliferation of news outlets, social media platforms, and online forums, it can be difficult for Jack to sift through conflicting narratives and focus on reliable, actionable information.

- **Trusted news sources:** Jack should rely on credible news outlets, government agencies, and expert organizations to stay informed about emerging global threats. Government agencies such as FEMA, the CDC, and the National Weather Service offer timely updates on disasters, health alerts, and safety protocols. By subscribing to their alerts and monitoring trusted news sources, Jack can ensure that his family receives up-to-date information without falling prey to misinformation.

- **Avoiding misinformation:** In times of crisis, misinformation can spread quickly, causing panic and confusion. Jack must teach his family how to evaluate the credibility of information by checking the sources, cross-referencing facts, and relying on official channels. Being skeptical of unverified reports and social media rumors will help his family make informed decisions without succumbing to fear-driven reactions.

Long-Term Impacts of Global Threats

Some global threats may not manifest immediately but could have long-term consequences that affect Jack's family over the course of years or even decades. These include economic instability, societal shifts, and long-term environmental changes. For Jack, preparing for these slow-burn crises is just as important as responding to sudden emergencies.

- **Economic instability:** Global financial markets are highly interdependent, meaning that a crisis in one region can trigger ripple effects worldwide. Jack should remain vigilant about economic trends, including inflation, market crashes, and rising debt levels. Long-term economic instability can lead to job losses, housing crises, and inflation, all of which can threaten Jack's ability to provide for his family. Building a financial safety net, including diversifying investments and stockpiling essential goods, will help Jack mitigate the impact of financial disruptions.
- **Societal shifts and migration:** As global threats such as climate change and war continue to reshape the world, Jack may see an increase in migration and population shifts. This could lead to crowded urban areas, strained public services, and rising crime rates. Jack must be prepared for the potential of living in a changing society, where competition for resources increases and social tensions rise.

Adapting Preparedness Plans to Evolving Threats

Finally, Jack needs to be proactive in adapting his family's preparedness plan to the evolving nature of global threats. What was sufficient five years ago may no longer apply today. Jack's family should regularly review and update their emergency plans, factoring in new risks, technological advancements, and changes to their local environment.

- **Regular risk assessments:** Jack should establish a routine for evaluating global threats. This could involve quarterly family meetings where they review their preparedness plans, assess new risks, and identify areas for improvement. By keeping a close eye on global developments, Jack ensures that his family's plan remains relevant and effective.
- **Flexibility and adaptability:** One of the most valuable qualities in long-term preparedness is the ability to adapt to new circumstances. Jack's family must be ready to modify their plans on the fly, whether that means finding new ways to generate energy, growing their own food, or adjusting their bug-in strategy. Flexibility will be the key to surviving in a rapidly changing world where new threats are constantly emerging.

Assessing new global threats is an ongoing process that requires vigilance, adaptability, and a proactive approach to preparedness. For Jack, staying ahead of these dangers means not only reacting to immediate crises but also thinking long-term, ensuring that his family is prepared for whatever the future may hold.

Building Resilience for Long-Term Crises

Building resilience for long-term crises requires both a proactive mindset and a systematic approach to preparedness. While immediate responses to disasters are essential, true resilience lies in the ability to endure prolonged periods of uncertainty and resource scarcity without succumbing to panic or exhaustion. Resilience isn't just about physical preparedness but also involves cultivating mental, emotional, and logistical strength. By developing these layers of resilience, you ensure that your family can face long-term crises—whether they are environmental, economic, or societal—with confidence and clarity.

Understanding the Nature of Long-Term Crises

Long-term crises differ from short-term emergencies in their duration and the cumulative toll they take on individuals and communities. These crises can last months or even years, with ongoing disruptions to daily life, supply chains, and infrastructure. Events such as economic collapse, prolonged pandemics, or widespread civil unrest can erode resources, strain mental and emotional capacities, and create significant uncertainty about the future.

Types of Long-Term Crises to Consider:

- **Economic crises:** Financial downturns, inflation, and unemployment can significantly impact a family's access to essentials such as food, healthcare, and housing.
- **Environmental crises:** Climate change and its associated effects, such as prolonged droughts, wildfires, and extreme weather patterns, can disrupt access to clean water, food, and safe shelter.
- **Pandemics:** The COVID-19 pandemic was a stark reminder of how a global health crisis can upend daily routines, strain healthcare systems, and lead to long-term economic and societal shifts.
- **Societal instability:** Political unrest, social upheaval, and large-scale migration caused by regional conflicts or natural disasters can destabilize even the most secure communities.

When preparing for long-term crises, it's essential to acknowledge that they will likely cause strain not just physically but also mentally and emotionally. Resilience, therefore, must be built across all these domains to ensure your family remains strong throughout the crisis.

Mental and Emotional Resilience

One of the most overlooked aspects of long-term crisis preparedness is the importance of mental and emotional resilience. Sustaining your family's morale, maintaining hope, and staying focused on solutions is key to surviving a prolonged crisis without burning out.

Strategies for Building Mental Resilience:

- **Routine and structure:** In the face of chaos, maintaining a daily routine can provide a sense of normalcy. Even during a prolonged crisis, establishing regular schedules for meals, work, and family time can reduce anxiety and foster a sense of control.
- **Focusing on what you can control:** During a crisis, it's easy to become overwhelmed by factors beyond your control. Training your family to focus on actionable tasks—such as managing resources, fortifying your home, or working on self-sufficiency projects—can alleviate feelings of helplessness.
- **Supporting emotional health:** Regularly talking about fears and concerns within the family and finding healthy outlets for stress, such as exercise or creative activities, are critical to maintaining emotional well-being over the long term.

Resource Management and Sustainability

In a long-term crisis, resource management becomes a central issue. Food, water, energy, and medical supplies may be scarce, so ensuring your family has a plan for sustainable resource use will be key to weathering the storm.

- **Stockpiling wisely:** Building a supply of essential items is crucial, but it's equally important to stockpile in a sustainable way. This means choosing items with long shelf lives, rotating supplies to prevent waste, and ensuring that each family member knows how to ration resources if necessary.
- **Water conservation and purification:** In a long-term crisis, access to clean water is critical. Installing a rainwater harvesting system or using purification methods can ensure a steady supply of drinkable water. Teach family members how to monitor water usage and conserve wherever possible, using greywater for non-potable needs such as irrigation.
- **Growing your own food:** Food shortages and supply chain disruptions are common during prolonged crises. Developing a home garden with nutrient-dense crops such as beans, greens, and root vegetables ensures your family has access to fresh, sustainable food. Involving your family in the garden also creates a sense of purpose and self-reliance during challenging times.
- **Energy independence:** Renewable energy sources like solar panels or wind turbines can be essential in long-term crises, where the power grid may be unreliable. Energy conservation practices, such as limiting the use of electronics, cooking with efficient methods, and insulating your home properly, can help extend your energy supplies.

Building Community Resilience

Resilience in the face of long-term crises doesn't have to be a solitary effort. In fact, building relationships with neighbors and community members can significantly improve your family's ability to cope with the challenges ahead.

Developing a Community Support System:

- **Skill-sharing:** Each household has different skills and resources to offer. By networking with neighbors, you can establish a skill-sharing system, where those with medical training, gardening knowledge, or mechanical expertise can help others.
- **Bartering and trading:** During prolonged crises, money may lose its value or become inaccessible. Bartering goods and services within your community allows everyone to access the supplies they need without relying on cash.
- **Group safety strategies:** A crisis can bring out the best in people, but it can also create security risks, as resources become scarce and tensions rise. Organizing neighborhood watch groups or collaborating on home fortification projects helps create a safer, more secure environment for all.

Continuous Learning and Adaptation

One of the most crucial components of building resilience for long-term crises is the willingness to adapt and continuously learn. No one can predict exactly how a crisis will unfold, so Jack must remain flexible, ready to pivot his plans as circumstances change.

- **Monitoring developments:** Stay informed about new technologies, government policies, and global trends that may affect your preparedness strategy. For example, advancements in renewable energy or home automation may offer new opportunities for self-sufficiency.
- **Learning from experience:** Whether it's reviewing past crises or learning from others' experiences, staying open to new information and adapting based on real-world examples will help refine Jack's strategy.
- **Practicing flexibility:** While having a robust plan in place is critical, Jack should also practice adaptability. This includes preparing the family to shift gears quickly, whether it's relocating temporarily, rationing supplies differently, or adjusting the strategy based on the evolving situation.

Building resilience for long-term crises is a holistic process. It's about preparing physically, mentally, emotionally, and logistically to endure whatever challenges come your way. With careful planning, resource management, and the right mindset, Jack's family will be well-equipped to thrive through prolonged adversity.

Planning for Financial Instability

Financial instability is one of the most insidious threats facing individuals and families during a long-term crisis. While economic downturns are often inevitable in global or local crises, you can take proactive steps to safeguard your family's financial well-being. Whether caused by job loss, market collapse, hyperinflation, or a breakdown of monetary systems, financial instability can create a ripple effect, impacting access to essential goods, services, and even shelter. Jack's focus, therefore, should be on building a strategy that not only shields his family from immediate financial shocks but also provides a framework for long-term economic resilience.

Diversifying Income Streams

One of the most important strategies to mitigate financial instability is diversifying income streams. Relying on a single source of income, such as a job or a business that could be affected by a crisis, leaves a family vulnerable. By having multiple income sources, Jack can reduce risk and maintain some level of financial security even if one income stream dries up.

Examples of Diversified Income Sources:

- **Side businesses or freelance work:** Jack and his family can start small ventures that capitalize on their skills, such as offering handyman services, gardening, or teaching skills online.
- **Investments in physical assets:** Diversifying into assets that hold their value during economic downturns, such as gold, silver, or real estate, can provide a hedge against inflation and currency devaluation.
- **Bartering and trading:** In a crisis where cash flow is limited or currency loses its value, bartering goods and services within the local community can offer an alternative means of exchange.

By focusing on alternative income streams that can function independently of the traditional economy, Jack reduces the impact of financial instability on his family.

Building an Emergency Savings Fund

Another critical pillar in planning for financial instability is establishing an emergency savings fund. This fund should be liquid, meaning easily accessible in times of need, and should cover at least six to twelve months of living expenses. The idea is to ensure that Jack's family can continue to pay for essentials such as food, utilities, and healthcare, even if their income is temporarily disrupted.

Key Principles for Building an Emergency Fund:

- **Prioritize savings:** Consistently set aside a percentage of income for savings, even if it means cutting back on non-essential expenditures.

- **Automate contributions:** Automating regular contributions to an emergency savings account helps build the fund without requiring Jack to actively think about it each month.
- **Keep it separate:** Ensure the emergency fund is not mingled with other savings or investment accounts to reduce the temptation of using it for non-emergency situations.

For Jack, an emergency fund serves as a buffer, providing peace of mind during uncertain times. It also allows him to respond more calmly and strategically in the face of financial instability.

Reducing Debt and Financial Obligations

During a crisis, debt can quickly become a burden. Interest rates may rise, making loan repayments more expensive, or income disruptions may make it difficult to meet monthly obligations. Therefore, reducing debt before a crisis hits—or strategically managing it during one—becomes crucial for long-term financial survival.

Steps for Managing Debt in a Crisis:

- **Prioritize high-interest debt:** Jack should focus on paying down high-interest loans, such as credit card debt, as quickly as possible. These types of debts can spiral out of control, especially when income becomes uncertain.
- **Negotiate with creditors:** In some cases, creditors may offer flexibility, such as payment deferrals or interest rate reductions, during times of financial hardship. It's essential to communicate with creditors early to explore these options.
- **Avoid taking on new debt:** While it may be tempting to rely on credit during a crisis, doing so only adds to long-term financial strain. Jack should aim to live within his means and avoid unnecessary financial obligations.

By reducing debt and limiting financial liabilities, Jack ensures that more of his family's resources are available to cover essential needs during a crisis.

Stockpiling Essential Goods

In a prolonged economic crisis, access to essential goods may become scarce or prohibitively expensive due to inflation. To mitigate this risk, Jack should consider stockpiling non-perishable goods, medical supplies, and other essentials. Not only does this ensure his family has access to necessary items, but it also provides a hedge against price increases caused by inflation or supply chain disruptions.

Goods to Prioritize in a Stockpile:

- **Food:** Canned and dry foods that have long shelf lives, such as beans, rice, and pasta, should form the basis of a food stockpile. Additionally, consider storing vitamins and supplements to ensure balanced nutrition.
- **Medical supplies:** Over-the-counter medications, first aid supplies, and prescription

medications (if possible) are essential in a long-term crisis where healthcare may become difficult to access.

- **Fuel and energy supplies:** Stockpiling propane, batteries, and firewood ensures that Jack's family can continue to cook, heat their home, and power essential devices if utilities are disrupted.

A well-rounded stockpile reduces reliance on fluctuating markets and protects Jack's family from shortages that may arise during periods of financial instability.

Developing Self-Sufficiency Skills

Financial instability often leads to inflated prices for goods and services, making it more important than ever to reduce dependency on external resources. Developing skills for self-sufficiency allows Jack's family to meet many of their own needs without relying on outside help or spending money on services they can perform themselves.

Key Self-Sufficiency Skills:

- **Gardening and food preservation:** Growing your own food and learning how to can, dry, or freeze it allows Jack's family to reduce grocery bills and rely on home-grown produce.
- **Basic home repairs:** Learning how to perform essential home maintenance tasks, such as plumbing repairs, carpentry, and electrical work, reduces the need to hire professionals.
- **Clothing repairs and alterations:** In a long-term crisis, buying new clothes may become a luxury. Knowing how to mend clothes or alter them for better fit ensures the family's clothing lasts longer.

By developing these skills, Jack's family can maintain a higher quality of life while minimizing their financial outlay during an extended crisis.

Safeguarding Investments and Retirement Funds

Finally, protecting investments and retirement funds is essential to ensuring long-term financial stability. Financial instability often leads to stock market fluctuations and declines in investment values, so it's important to adopt a diversified strategy to safeguard against these risks.

Investment Strategies for Uncertain Times:

- **Diversify across asset classes:** Instead of relying solely on stocks, Jack should consider diversifying his investments into bonds, real estate, commodities, and precious metals. This spreads risk across various markets and provides a buffer if one sector collapses.
- **Consider conservative investments:** While growth-oriented investments may be tempting, conservative options such as government bonds or savings accounts offer stability in times of crisis.

- **Stay informed:** Regularly reviewing investment portfolios and staying informed about market trends can help Jack make timely decisions to protect his family's financial future.

By taking a thoughtful and conservative approach to his investments, Jack ensures that his family's long-term savings are protected, even in the face of economic instability.

In summary, planning for financial instability requires a holistic approach that includes building emergency savings, reducing debt, stockpiling essential goods, and developing self-sufficiency skills. With careful planning and a focus on resilience, Jack can ensure his family remains financially secure throughout any prolonged crisis.

Updating Your Plan for Technological Advances

In an ever-evolving world, technology plays a pivotal role in shaping how we prepare for and respond to long-term crises. Ignoring technological advances when planning for emergency preparedness could leave Jack and his family vulnerable. As new tools and systems emerge, incorporating these innovations into the family's crisis plan is crucial to ensuring resilience. Whether it's in communication, energy storage, or security, keeping abreast of the latest technological developments can be the difference between thriving and merely surviving in a prolonged emergency.

Leveraging Advances in Communication Technology

One of the most critical areas where technology has significantly evolved is communication. Gone are the days when families relied solely on landlines or two-way radios. Now, Jack can incorporate modern communication technologies that not only improve range and clarity but also enable better coordination in emergencies.

Key technological upgrades for communication:

- **Satellite Phones:** Unlike mobile networks, which can fail during disasters, satellite phones provide reliable communication no matter where Jack's family is located. These phones connect directly to satellites, making them an excellent backup during emergencies when cellular towers are down or overloaded.
- **Mesh Networks:** This technology allows for decentralized communication by connecting devices directly without relying on central hubs like cell towers or routers. In an urban environment, mesh networks can be a lifeline, enabling Jack's family and neighbors to communicate securely and privately, even when traditional networks are down.
- **Emergency Communication Apps:** Some apps are designed to work offline, using Bluetooth or Wi-Fi Direct to relay messages between users within a certain range. These tools are particularly useful for short-range communication when the internet is not available.

By integrating these advancements into the family's crisis response plan, Jack ensures that his family remains connected during high-stress situations, with access to the latest, most reliable communication technologies.

Enhanced Security Through Smart Home Technology

Technological advances have also revolutionized home security systems. Smart home technologies allow Jack to create a comprehensive defense system that not only monitors external threats but can also be managed remotely.

Key upgrades in security technology:

- **Smart Surveillance Systems:** With the ability to remotely access live footage from security cameras, Jack can monitor his home even if he's not physically present. Features like motion detection, night vision, and two-way audio enhance the security system's functionality, allowing immediate responses to any threat.
- **Automated Locks and Access Control:** Traditional locks are becoming obsolete in the face of more sophisticated automated systems. Smart locks enable Jack to remotely lock or unlock doors, provide temporary access to trusted individuals, and monitor entry points from a distance.
- **AI-Powered Intrusion Detection:** Artificial Intelligence can now differentiate between common, non-threatening activities and potential intrusions. Advanced security systems use AI to analyze patterns, significantly reducing false alarms while giving Jack real-time updates on suspicious behavior around his home.

Incorporating these technologies into Jack's long-term plan enhances home security, making it more adaptable and responsive to new threats.

Renewable Energy and Efficient Power Storage

Energy independence is critical during long-term crises, and recent technological advances in renewable energy and energy storage offer numerous benefits for families like Jack's. Solar panels and wind turbines are becoming more efficient and affordable, but it's the innovations in energy storage that truly revolutionize off-grid living.

Key upgrades in renewable energy:

- **Next-Generation Solar Panels:** Advances in photovoltaic technology have led to the creation of more efficient solar panels that can generate more electricity with less sunlight. Jack can now install solar panels that are smaller, yet produce the same or higher energy output as older models, making them ideal for homes with limited roof space.
- **Battery Storage Systems:** Modern battery storage systems, like Tesla's Powerwall, allow families to store excess energy generated by renewable sources. In a crisis, Jack's family can rely on these stored reserves to power critical systems like lighting, refrigeration, and communication.

- **Smart Energy Management Systems:** These systems monitor energy consumption and automatically optimize power usage in the home. Jack can reduce waste and ensure that essential systems are prioritized during an emergency, extending the life of his power reserves and ensuring uninterrupted service for vital functions.

By updating the family's energy plan to incorporate these technologies, Jack can enhance their energy independence, ensuring resilience in the face of power grid failures.

Adaptable Water Purification Systems

Water is a fundamental resource during any crisis, and advancements in water purification technology allow Jack's family to access clean, safe drinking water from a variety of sources. Modern filtration systems have become more compact, portable, and effective at removing a broader range of contaminants.

Innovations in water purification:

- **Portable Reverse Osmosis Systems:** These systems are now more compact and portable, enabling Jack's family to purify water from sources that may have high levels of contaminants, including heavy metals, bacteria, and viruses.
- **Solar-Powered Water Purification:** Technological advances in solar-powered purification allow families to use the sun's energy to purify water in remote locations. Jack can invest in systems that combine UV and filtration technologies, ensuring water safety even when access to traditional power is limited.
- **UV Water Purifiers:** Small, handheld UV purifiers can disinfect water quickly and efficiently, making them ideal for both emergency situations and everyday use when local water supplies are compromised.

By updating the family's water plan to include these modern purification systems, Jack can ensure access to clean drinking water in almost any situation.

Financial Technologies for Crisis Preparedness

Financial stability in times of crisis goes beyond traditional banking and investment systems. Technological innovations have given rise to new methods of storing, transferring, and safeguarding wealth during periods of instability.

Emerging financial technologies:

- **Cryptocurrency and Blockchain:** Cryptocurrencies like Bitcoin offer a decentralized form of wealth storage that can be accessed globally, even if traditional banks are shut down. Blockchain technology ensures secure, transparent transactions, which can be vital in ensuring Jack's family's financial safety during economic collapse or hyperinflation.
- **Mobile Payment Systems:** Peer-to-peer mobile payment systems like Venmo or Pay-

Pal have evolved to include offline payment features, allowing Jack to send or receive funds even when internet access is spotty.

- **Gold-Backed Digital Currencies:** Some new financial technologies combine the stability of precious metals with the convenience of digital payments. Digital currencies backed by gold ensure that Jack's wealth retains its value during economic downturns, while still allowing him to make quick transactions in times of need.

Incorporating these financial technologies into Jack's long-term preparedness strategy ensures his family's access to wealth and resources, even during the most severe financial crises.

The Importance of Regularly Updating Technological Plans

Technological advancements evolve rapidly, and what might be cutting-edge today could become obsolete in just a few years. Therefore, Jack must adopt a mindset of continuous evaluation and updates to ensure that his family's preparedness plan is always equipped with the latest and most reliable tools. Regularly reviewing innovations in security, energy, communication, and financial technologies will help Jack stay ahead of emerging threats and crises, ensuring long-term resilience for his family.

By updating his crisis plan with the latest technologies, Jack can enhance his family's chances of thriving, even in the most challenging of times. These innovations provide security, energy independence, and financial stability, all of which are critical to weathering long-term crises.

Learning from Real-World Bug-In Case Studies

The best way to prepare for a crisis is to learn from those who have already lived through one. Real-world bug-in scenarios provide invaluable lessons in resilience, resourcefulness, and adaptability. Whether it's natural disasters, pandemics, or civil unrest, these case studies offer practical insights into what works, what doesn't, and how individuals and families can improve their own preparedness plans. Studying these experiences helps Jack understand the realities of bugging in, beyond theoretical strategies, allowing him to refine his family's plan to ensure long-term survival.

Case Study: The Pandemic Lockdown

One of the most relevant and recent bug-in scenarios was the global COVID-19 pandemic. The sudden and widespread lockdowns forced millions of people worldwide to shelter in place, providing an unprecedented case study in how families can manage long-term isolation and supply shortages. For Jack, this example offers lessons on the importance of planning for extended periods without external resources.

Key takeaways from pandemic lockdowns:

- **Supply Chain Disruptions:** During the early stages of the pandemic, many families experienced shortages of essential goods like food, water, and personal protective equipment. Jack's bug-in plan should account for these kinds of disruptions by ensuring that his family has adequate stockpiles of non-perishable food, water, and medical supplies.

- **Mental Health Strain:** Long periods of isolation took a toll on people's mental well-being, with stress, anxiety, and depression becoming widespread issues. This reinforces the importance of not only physical preparedness but also psychological resilience. Jack can integrate mental health strategies, such as daily routines, entertainment, and communication with loved ones, into his family's plan to mitigate the emotional impact of isolation.

- **Home-Based Education and Work:** Many families found themselves suddenly adapting to remote work and schooling, which highlighted the need for a stable internet connection, digital devices, and a comfortable workspace. Jack's bug-in strategy should include provisions for continued education and employment in case his family needs to shelter in place for an extended period.

This real-world case study demonstrates the necessity of planning for both physical and emotional challenges, making Jack's preparedness approach more holistic and adaptable to long-term crises.

Case Study: Natural Disasters in New Orleans

The aftermath of Hurricane Katrina in 2005 is another critical case study. Thousands of residents were forced to bug in due to flooded streets and lack of evacuation options. While the government response was slow and uncoordinated, individuals who had prepared for long-term crises were able to survive the worst of the disaster.

Key takeaways from Hurricane Katrina:

- **Water and Food Scarcity:** After the floodwaters destroyed infrastructure, access to clean water and food became a major challenge for survivors. Many were left without potable water for days. For Jack, this highlights the importance of a robust water filtration and purification system, as well as the need for long-term food storage. Emergency rations should be rotated regularly, and water storage should be sufficient for at least several weeks.

- **Breakdown of Law and Order:** The collapse of local law enforcement led to looting, violence, and general chaos in some areas. Jack can take this into account by bolstering his family's home security with reinforced doors, secure windows, and even weapons, if appropriate. Learning from Katrina, it's clear that personal safety becomes a top priority during a prolonged bug-in scenario.

- **Community Support:** One surprising outcome of the disaster was how communities came together to support one another. Neighborhoods that had strong ties were able to pool resources, share information, and offer mutual aid. Jack should consider establishing connections with his neighbors and local networks before a crisis hits. Building these relationships will make it easier to share resources and collaborate on survival strategies during an emergency.

This case study offers a stark reminder of the importance of water, security, and community support in a crisis, helping Jack refine his bug-in plan to better meet these challenges.

Case Study: Argentina's Economic Collapse

In the early 2000s, Argentina experienced a severe economic collapse that left much of the population in poverty, with skyrocketing inflation and limited access to basic goods. For families like Jack's, who might face economic instability in the future, this case study offers lessons in long-term financial resilience and survival during periods of hyperinflation.

Key takeaways from Argentina's economic collapse:

- **Bartering and Alternative Economies:** With the collapse of the formal economy, many people turned to bartering for goods and services. Jack can learn from this by stockpiling not only essential supplies for his family but also items that could be used for trade, such as alcohol, fuel, batteries, or even medical supplies. Understanding the value of bartering in times of economic hardship could be critical for Jack's long-term preparedness.
- **Self-Sufficiency:** Many Argentine families survived by growing their own food and raising livestock. This reinforces the need for Jack to incorporate gardening and animal husbandry into his preparedness plan. By producing his own food, Jack can avoid dependence on external food supply chains, which are vulnerable to economic instability.
- **Personal Safety:** Crime rates surged during Argentina's collapse as people became desperate. For Jack, this highlights the importance of home fortification and security. Learning from Argentina, it's clear that Jack should prioritize self-defense training, secure storage for valuables, and possibly even relocation to a safer area if the crisis worsens.

Argentina's collapse serves as a powerful example of how long-term crises can reshape economies and daily life. By studying this case, Jack can better prepare for similar economic challenges that could arise in the future.

Case Study: Urban Bug-In During the Syrian Civil War

The Syrian Civil War has led to one of the most devastating humanitarian crises in modern history, with millions of people either fleeing as refugees or bugging in under siege. For those who stayed behind, survival depended on creative solutions, adaptability, and strong community ties.

Key takeaways from the Syrian Civil War:

- **Adapting to Scarcity:** People living in besieged cities like Aleppo had to survive with limited access to food, water, and medical care. Many families relied on urban gardening, scavenging, and recycling to stretch their resources. Jack can learn from this by implementing small-scale gardening projects and teaching his family how to identify local resources that can be repurposed or reused.

- **Strength in Community:** In the most severe conditions, families relied heavily on their neighbors for protection, resource sharing, and emotional support. This reinforces the need for Jack to build a strong local network. Whether it's through formal neighborhood organizations or informal community groups, having a supportive network can be a life-saving asset during a bug-in scenario.

- **Mental Resilience:** The trauma of living in a war zone took a heavy toll on the mental health of survivors. However, those who maintained a sense of purpose, structure, and hope fared better psychologically. Jack should incorporate mental resilience strategies into his plan, ensuring that his family stays grounded through routines, goals, and mutual support, even during extended periods of crisis.

Learning from the experiences of Syrian families, Jack can enhance his family's preparedness by focusing on resourcefulness, community building, and mental strength.